Perfect Phrases for
Sales Presentations

Perfect Phrases for Sales Presentations

**Hundreds of Ready-to-Use Phrases
for Delivering Powerful
Presentations That Close
Every Sale**

Linda Eve Diamond

New York Chicago San Francisco Lisbon
London Madrid Mexico City Milan New Delhi
San Juan Seoul Singapore Sydney Toronto

The **McGraw·Hill** Companies

1 2 3 4 5 6 7 8 9 0   FGR/FGR   0 1 0 9

ISBN: 978-0-07-163453-3
MHID: 0-07-163453-3

This book is printed on acid-free paper.

McGraw-Hill books are available at special quantity discounts to use as premiums and sales promotions, or for use in corporate training programs. To contact a representative please e-mail us at bulksales@mcgraw-hill.com.

Contents

Preface   xi

Who Can Use This Book?   xii

Book Map   xii

An Emphasis on Listening   xviii

Enter Here   xix

Acknowledgments   xxi

Part One: Foundations   1

Chapter 1: Presentation Basics   3

Image   3

What You Say   5

How You Say It   6

What You Hear   7

Enthusiasm   8

Knowledge   8

Skill   9

Knowing When to Let Go   10

Contents

Chapter 2: First Impressions   13

Your Office   14
Your Web Site   14
Your Overall Web Presence   15
On Paper   16
Why Choose You?   16

Part Two: The Presentation   19

Chapter 3: The First Step   21

Cold Calls   23
Warm Calls   27
Closing the Cold or Warm Call   31
Hot Calls   33
Networking in Person   36
Networking Online   41

Chapter 4: Preparation   45

Are You Ready?   46
Do You Know the Competition?   50
Preappointment Questions   52
Foot-in-the-Door Questions   54
When You've Been Referred   57

Chapter 5: Presentation Pointers   61

Essential Presentation Pointers   62
Getting Their Attention   65
Putting Prospects at Ease   68

Contents

Timing   70

Engaging the Prospect   73

Chapter 6: Focused Phrases for Any Presentation   75

Selling Products   77

Selling Services   80

Accentuate the Positive   83

The Competitive Edge   85

Chapter 7: Language, Style, and Creativity   89

Winning Words and Phrases   90

Avoid These Imperfect Phrases   93

Insider Language   95

Metaphorically Speaking   97

Chapter 8: Always Be Listening!   103

Listen for Success   104

Ask Good Big-Picture Questions   107

Ask Good Basic Questions   110

Show that You're Listening   113

Encourage Questions   115

When You Don't Know the Answer   117

Chapter 9: Answering Objections and Closing the Sale   119

Hidden or Unclear Objections   121

Objections: General   124

Objections as Opportunities   128

Contents

Objections to Price   130
Presentation Closing   134
Closing the Deal   137
Closing the Deal: Asking for "Yes"   140
Closing the Deal: The A or B Close   141
Closing the Deal: Touching Sense and Emotion   143
Follow Up to Close the Sale   146
Feel-Good Closing Words   148
The Absolute Wrong Fit   150

Chapter 10: Follow-Up and Beyond   153

Follow Up after the Sale   154
Ask for Feedback   156
Ask for Referrals and Testimonials   158

Part Three: Ongoing Development   161

Chapter 11: Eleven Final Thoughts on Learning   163

Practice Active Learning   164
Study, Learn, and Practice Public Speaking   164
Strengthen Your Writing Skills   165
Always Be Learning to Listen   167
Listen, Watch, and Read the Works of Great Motivators   167
Keep Up to Speed with Your Professional Development   168
Study, Watch, Learn, and Practice Sales Skills   169
Keep Up with Technology   170
Keep Up a Strong Knowledge Base   170
Use the Buddy System   171
Be a Student of Life, School, and Beyond   172

Contents

Chapter 12: Your *Perfect Phrases*   175

Have You Made *Perfect* Notes?   175
What Makes a Phrase *Perfect*?   175
A *Perfect* Brainstorm   176
A *Perfect* Buddy   177
More *Perfect Phrase* Tips   177

Conclusion   181

About the Author   185

Preface

Welcome to *Perfect Phrases for Sales Presentations*. As always, these phrases are guidelines. Some can be used directly or with only slight modifications, and others may inspire a new, creative phrase that's pinpointed for your audience and purpose. While some phrases will become standard parts of your presentation, a successful salesperson is always continually refining his or her pitch, and the most successful presentations are created and refined with each prospect's individual needs, interests, and values in mind.

Because any perfect phrase can be the one to intrigue or entice a potential prospect or to close the sale, I've added a special section to this edition of *Perfect Phrases* called "Your *Perfect Phrases.*" This new section is designed to assist you in creating more fresh, relevant *perfect phrases* as you continue to refine and pinpoint your presentations over time. But first you'll find numerous phrases that lead you from getting through the door through closing and follow-up.

Whether you are an experienced sales professional or new to the field, I hope you'll find that these *perfect phrases* are helpful as you develop and hone your sales presentations.

Who Can Use This Book?

Perfect Phrases for Sales Presentations is an easy-to-carry, easily referenced resource for anyone who gives sales presentations. Whatever your business, whatever your goals, bottom lines depend on gaining buy-in, continued interest, and referrals from potential clients and customers. This book is designed for those who specialize in sales, whether retail or business-to-business, online or face-to-face, and those who sell products, services, or ideas. This book is useful for those with the title of *salesperson* but also for small- and large-business owners, and the self-employed who rely on themselves for sales and/or marketing efforts.

The sales-success mindsets and phrases are designed, for the most part, to cross industry needs. If, however, some do not apply to your industry, they can be easily adapted to suit your needs. (Please accept the broad use of the words *clients* and *customers*. I often refer to clients and customers interchangeably.)

Book Map

Since a sales presentation is only great if you can get in front of the prospect, *Perfect Phrases for Sales Presentations* begins at the beginning—establishing a relationship. From there, the book takes you through helpful phrases from setting up your presentation through closing and follow-up.

Part One: Foundations

Before you even think about building your sales presentation, you want to be sure that you are working on a solid foundation.

Chapters 1 and 2 address the issues of your foundation and your image, which may be the first impressions prospects will have of you—before they've even met you. Your presentation begins with how you present yourself. Who are you as a salesperson? What is your image? What attitude do you project? Beyond choosing the right words, are you comfortable with yourself and knowledgeable about your product or service? Do you have some understanding of human nature and strong communications skills? Your image is another aspect of your foundation to consider, and so is your reputation. Even if you already have a strong foundation, you may want to read Part One to self-assess and consider whether any part of your image, outlook, or style needs strengthening to build the most successful presentations.

Part Two: The Presentation

Chapter 3 addresses the first steps to finding and cultivating potential clients. A great presentation begins with finding and reaching out to prospects and preparing your presentation. Your initial contacts—such as cold calling, following up with warm leads and hot prospects, networking in person, and networking online—establish a relationship, open the door, and set the stage for your presentation. Chapter 4 addresses preparation. Preparation requires some self-questioning and readiness checks and good questions to ask either your potential client or your referral source. The more you know going in, the more you can target your presentation. Once you've identified and reached out to prospects and prepared, it's time for the presentation.

Chapter 5 begins with some basic presentation pointers and then flows into mindsets and phrases for the two most important goals for the start of your presentation: getting their attention and putting them at ease. What else is important for a *perfect* start? Never underestimate the importance of great time management and clear, concise communication about time. The time to think about timing is when you prepare the presentation, as you begin and throughout. Timing phrases are included here to stress the importance of clearly identifying and sticking to your time frame. When your audience is concerned about time, it'll be distracted. Communicating about time helps people to relax. Engaging them in interactive communication, to some degree, during the presentation also helps to put them at ease and invest them in what you're saying. The final pointers in this chapter offer a few simple phrases to engage your audience in your presentation.

Chapter 6 offers focused mindsets and phrases for selling products and others for selling services, although there is some crossover, especially if you are selling a product that is associated with a service. Other focused phrases include those that accentuate the positive aspects of your product or service and those that would help you to manage and common ways to diplomatically—without insulting your competition—show your competitive edge.

Chapter 7 speaks to language. Not every phrase has to be crafted with care to be perfect to put the prospect at ease, elicit helpful information, or make the sale. And not all *perfect phrases* use creative language or concepts—but language does have a powerful impact when it comes to sales. Some words tend to create positive feelings, whereas others bring up negative feelings. When we use jargon, we leave people on the outside.

Beyond jargon, "insider" language can flag someone as an "outsider." Language can paint pictures. In sales, we paint pictures with words and use stories, metaphors, or words that persuade, and the prospect will "see" not only the benefits but also the outcomes. Chapter 8 speaks to listening. While this is a book of phrases, it would be a disservice not to include listening. While this book has a listening thread throughout, this chapter focuses on phrases that deal specifically with listening. Of course, listening involves putting aside even your most brilliant phrases long enough to hear the prospect's interests and concerns; you also can use phrases to encourage speaking and show that you're listening and to ask and encourage questions. What if you encourage questions but don't know the answers? It's likely to be a question that will come up again, so consider that being faced with a difficult question is a good time to learn. The presentation itself is more than what you say; it's how you say it and how you listen to responses, questions, and feedback.

Chapter 9 is the longest chapter because there's no sale without the close, and closing the deal is an art in itself. No matter how strong, comprehensive, and convincing your presentation, it takes a strong closer to make the sale. From hidden or unclear objections to general objections to specific objections, this chapter offers phrases that lead to the close. Your sales presentation may be one-on-one, or it may be a more formal presentation in front of a group. If your presentation is formal, the presentation itself needs a powerful close, even though the conversation will continue—hopefully to the close of the deal.

No presentation should fizzle at the end and simply roll into a conversation where prospects wonder if there's more to come in the way of slides or the formal portion of your presentation. For this reason, presentation closings are included. Closing lines may be found throughout the "Objections" sections and through the "Closing the Deal" sections from basic to specific styles. The presentation also should close with some positive words that make people feel good about their investments with you, so the "Feel-Good Closing Words" section is important too.

The final section of Chapter 9 is "The Absolute Wrong Fit." Not every product or service is for every person at every time. This is not a reflection on you, but how you accept and handle these situations does reflect on you. Your response to these situations may earn you a reputation as pushy, or it may earn you referrals. Some sales are tough, but some are just impossible. Use the phrases at the close of Chapter 9 to build goodwill, and save your time for prospects who will be interested in what you have to offer.

Chapter 10 addresses following up and asking for feedback or referrals. Follow-up may not apply in certain situations, but when it does, it's often overlooked and undervalued. It can lead to additional sales and referrals. Whether you're selling products or services, choices are often made based on relationships, personalities, and trust. Your presentation is where you'll build that trust. Bringing in a client or making a sale has little impact if clients back out or return your products. Beyond ensuring a solid sale and opening up a potential for referrals, following up shows that you care about the relationship.

The presentation itself should be seen as a process, not an isolated event. Like a tennis swing, the swing itself—or the presentation—won't have the same power or effectiveness if you're not properly positioned first and ready for a smooth follow-through.

Part Three: Ongoing Development

Selling is an art and a skill that should be honed continually, and there is no lack of resources for honing that skill. Beyond continuing to develop and polish selling skills, any good salesperson keeps in touch with changes in his or her industry, with changes in the business climate overall, and with what the competition is offering. Ongoing development—in areas including speaking, writing, listening, and sales—allows you to be at your best and to show potential clients that you're in the thick of things and have the knowledge to offer them the very best for their specific needs. Chapter 11 has 11 sections, "Eleven Final Thoughts on Learning":

1. Active learning
2. Speaking
3. Writing
4. Listening
5. Motivation
6. Professional development
7. Sales skills
8. Technology
9. A strong knowledge base
10. The buddy system
11. Being a student of life, school, and beyond

Chapter 12 focuses on finding your *perfect phrases,* suggesting ways not only to recall and incorporate phrases from this book but also to create your own. It offers suggestions for taking notes, brainstorming, and using the buddy system to create more *perfect phrases.* Of course, most *perfect phrases* are positive phrases, so the final reminder of the section is about using *perfectly* positive language as you develop and practice your phrases.

An Emphasis on Listening

Even though this is a book of *perfect phrases,* I include a chapter on listening because I believe that no sales book should be without it. I write and speak about listening, and listening is an essential skill for salespeople. I include here phrases to encourage the client or customer to speak and phrases to show that you're listening and to clarify what you've heard. Of course, the best listening "phrase" is silence. So, beyond *perfect phrases,* this book offers advice on one of the most powerful things any salesperson can do to turn prospects into happy customers—listen!

Finding the *perfect phrases* for your sales presentations will increase your sales, but so will speaking less and listening more. As you read and hone your own *perfect phrases,* always remember that even with the *perfect phrases,* great salespeople listen to learn what concerns, inspires, and motivates a prospect and, ultimately, what this individual or company representative wants. Only by listening will you learn what people really want. Beyond hearing valuable information, you'll also be creating a bond by listening. If you want to forge a bond with someone, listen. The potential client will trust you only if you show that you truly understand that person's needs, and as any human being in any interaction, most of us like to speak to someone who is genuinely listening.

Practice equally your *perfect phrases* and your *perfect listening* to generate more sales and continue to build a strong base of happy customers.

Enter Here

Your willingness to learn and expand your expertise and knowledge of sales presentations—picking up *Perfect Phrases for Sales Presentations* and other books targeted to skill enhancement—is a testament to your ability to be highly successful. Use or modify the phrases in this book, and consider the mindsets behind them. If you're ready to infuse your presentations with *perfect phrases* and delve into the sales-success mindsets behind them, *enter here....*

Acknowledgments

I'd like to thank Jeff Novick, Walter Ladden, and Clemente Toglia, who talked to me as I wrote this book about their sales careers and the importance of loving what you do and what it means to be a trusted friend to clients, customers, prospects, and colleagues. They care for their customers with *perfect* heart and humor.

And, as always, I'd like to express my gratitude to my *perfect* editor Donya Dickerson and McGraw-Hill for including my work in the *Perfect Phrases* series!

Part One

Foundations

Chapter 1

Presentation Basics

"Sales are contingent upon the attitude of the salesman, not the attitude of the prospect."

—W. Clement Stone

Before you even begin to prepare your presentation, take a look at how you present yourself. You—not just your product or service—are a central part of your presentations. Your image, your enthusiasm, your whole way of being will be linked, in the prospect's mind, to what you are selling. Sales are often based on information, skill, and knowledge, but buying is usually emotional and is influenced by the enthusiasm and personality of the salesperson. *You*—your image, your attitude, your belief in the product or service you represent— make the sale.

Image

While we often say that a product or service is so outstanding that it sells itself, that's rarely the reality. Price and quality are factors when making purchasing decisions, but we all know that image sells. As consumers, our decisions are affected by the company's image, the salesperson's style and approach, and our comfort level with that salesperson. Image and relationship factors very often have as much to do with the sale as the price, quality, or convenience of what we're buying. Consumer surveys repeatedly show customer service at the top of the list in terms of what prospective customers value most when making a purchasing decision. We value the knowledge and comfort of knowing that we will be taken good care of if anything goes wrong. While we appreciate companies that build an image based on low price, high convenience, environmental friendliness, or a fun shopping experience, we still value service.

Know your market, your strengths, and your limitations. Know what your image is, and do what you can to create and maintain a good image both for yourself and for your company. What's your company's image? What's your personal image? Does your personal image match your company's image—and do you project the look and attitude that are most attractive to your target market? Your personal image ideally would match—or at least not clash with—the company's professional image. If your company's image is fun, smile. If it's environmental friendliness and your car is a gas guzzler, you won't seem sincere. While the words you choose are always an important consideration, they are also a part of the image you project, so pay close attention to the words you use. Are they positive? Do they paint pictures? Do they seem pushy or "salesy"? Be aware of the image you're projecting.

Your office, Web site, and overall online presence all establish an impression of you that either strengthens or weakens your presentation before you even walk into the room. Your reputation also precedes you when you make a presentation. What are people saying about you? People will be likely to see the comments you publicize, and they'll also be likely to speak to people or read commentaries or reviews that you wouldn't publicize.

What You Say

The goal of *Perfect Phrases for Sales Presentations* is to offer techniques and phrases that will enhance your presentations. Remember, though, that the best phrases are the ones that show you know your stuff—your product or service, your industry, *and* your client's industry—and that you know how to listen to your client's needs. After all, how else could you meet those needs?

A few things to remember about what you say:

- Be honest and be consistent. Nothing means more than your word. If the truth loses a sale, this was not the right customer for you at this time.
- Be artful, when you can, in your use of language—but never in expressing what is true.
- People won't remember every word you say, but they will remember the things that are most important to them—and they'll remember how you make them feel.
- Always be able to back up what you say.
- Always follow through with promises.
- If you make an error, own up to it immediately.
- Use humor, but never use it to anyone's detriment.
- Even if you don't say the *perfect phrase*, if you're showing interest in understanding and meeting the client's needs, you'll be making a good impression.

How You Say It

Pay attention to your speaking style, and remember that it's not always what you say but how you say it. You might say the *perfect phrase*, but if you sound desperate for the sale, impatient, or condescending, your phrase is no longer perfect at all.

Watch your tone. No matter how badly you want a sale, be careful not to sound desperate. If the sense is that the presentation is about your need to make a sale, your prospect is going to be far less interested in listening. Your tone should be one of "How can I help you?" Remember that your goal should be to do the best job that you can and then to follow through to see that your promise was delivered. The end result is a sale, but when you're in front of clients, always remember to focus on the goal of meeting their goals. By doing that, you'll meet your own.

Your attitude should be one of assurance that you can help—and honesty if you realize that you cannot. If your product or service is the wrong fit, you will gain more in the long run by being honest and giving a referral to someone else than by continuing to solicit a soon-to-be-unhappy customer. Both the customer and the person to whom you refer the customer will tell the story of your honesty and good business practices.

In speaking, also watch your pace. Fast-talking salespeople have a reputation for dishonesty. You might be meticulously honest in business, but if you're talking fast, certain prospects will feel unnerved or lose trust. Another thing about fast talkers is that they lose people without realizing it. Especially if your information is complex or new to the client, pay very careful attention to your pace, going slowly and inviting questions.

The most important point, though, about how you say things, comes back to your overall attitude and belief about your product or service. Are you enthusiastic about it? Do you genuinely believe in it and feel passionate about telling people about it? If you're selling something that doesn't interest or excite you—or something that you don't feel good about— you'll find it hard to achieve success. Sales has often been called a transfer of enthusiasm. I'm highly unlikely to be enthusiastic about what you're selling if you're not! Let your passion, your enthusiasm, and your overall good feeling about what you do and what you offer shine through! That kind of positive energy—if it's put behind something that really makes sense or captures the prospect's imagination—is hard to resist.

What You Hear

What you hear is as important as what you say. In fact, in a sales situation, it's more important. You need to listen for objections and desires—spoken and unspoken—and ask questions that encourage people not only to state but also to explore what it is they're looking for. The emphasis on listening, as you read on, is practical advice for listening to specific points that relate to the sale.

Another thing to keep in mind about listening, overall, is that it not only gives you the information you need to close the sale, but it also helps you to build a solid, ongoing client relationship. Along the way, you may hear more of a prospect's needs, concerns, and stories than those that relate to your immediate interests. Pay attention and show empathy and interest. Even if something you hear doesn't relate directly to the sale, listen attentively and respond with care. Don't be steadfast in taking in what clearly relates to the sale and blocking out what seems irrelevant to you. Part of developing ongoing relationships in sales is bonding and building trust. Don't see only dollar signs when you look at your prospect and hear only those things that directly affect the bottom line—see a human being—and *listen*.

Enthusiasm

Sales famously has been called a "transfer of enthusiasm." If you love what you do and feel good about your product or service, people will feel that energy and be interested in hearing more. Even in a tough economy, even with tight budgets, money is still being spent. We spend based on need, want, and emotion, and we spend because someone piques our interest and inspires us to see an outcome based on investing in the product or service being sold. The salesperson who comes to a presentation with enthusiasm has an edge over the one who comes in without a smile and presents clients with dry facts about which he or she seems disinterested. Beyond the enthusiasm around the product or service itself, remember that customers also encounter so many people who aren't enthusiastic about their lives and work that they are drawn to and interested in people who are. Beyond a general good feeling, I'd be hard pressed to become excited about your widget if you're not enthusiastic in your presentation. You become just another salesperson, and your widget becomes just another widget.

Knowledge

You can be brimming with personality and enthusiasm, but if you don't have knowledge about your industry, your company, your product or service, and how it may apply to your average prospect, you're lost. You're not only lost, but you also look and sound lost, which won't gain anyone's confidence. You don't have to have all the answers, and it's perfectly respectable to say that you don't know something. (In fact, people appreciate the honesty and the effort when you offer to find the correct answer or the missing information.) However, without a strong knowledge base, your confidence and enthusiasm mean nothing.

Skill

Beyond enthusiasm and knowledge, great salespeople hone their selling skills and continually tighten and refine their approaches to clients and potential clients and their presentations. Here, you'll consider some of the mindsets behind sales success and some *perfect phrases*. This is all part of skill building. So is refining your speaking style, practicing your presentation, and refining and integrating your *perfect phrases* into your presentation and as part of your natural conversation with clients and prospects. You can learn sales skills from books, CDs, DVDs, mentors, observation, seminars, lectures, articles, and Web sites, but the only way to develop your skills is to put them into practice.

Skilled salespeople are not only knowledgeable and enthusiastic, but they also know how to share and elicit information and make people feel comfortable, and they understand human psychology and what motivates people to buy. Skilled salespeople understand emotion, desire, fear, envy, ego—all the things that affect our choice of whether or not to invest in any given product or service.

Knowing When to Let Go

Let's consider for a moment the sales that got away. Were they all potentially good sales? Or did you know, in certain situations, that it was simply a bad fit and was time to walk away? Before you give up on a prospect, be the problem solver, and remember that most yes's follow a series of no's. But sometimes the product or service is a bad fit for the prospect, and you know you cannot fulfill the *perfect* promises and guarantees that would make this a satisfied customer. If this is the case, the *perfect* pitch is destined to hit a sour note. If it's a bad fit, tell the truth. Beyond building goodwill, you'll save yourself valuable time that you could be using with other clients and prospects.

Here's a true story about the *perfect* sale *never* made:

An older couple was enticed by a promotion for high-tech services. They called in a salesperson fully ready to buy. The salesperson, Bob, explained everything. They said, "But that's different from how we've always done things." Bob agreed and pointed out, gingerly, that most people like the new ways, but he could see their discomfort. The three of them had a long, philosophical talk about change. Bob smiled warmly and said, "You're not ready for this, and you wouldn't be happy." He recommended that they not make the purchase. They thanked him. They hugged him. They tell the story on a regular basis, and many of the people they speak to are more inclined to change than they are. Of course, they happily pass along Bob's number. Bob, by choosing not to even try to close, made a number of sales. If he had pushed to close that sale—and he could have—he would have had a canceled sale and no referrals. Sometimes, the *perfect phrase* is, "I understand your position and your concerns, and I agree. This may not be the best thing for you right now."

Chapter 2

First Impressions

"I don't like that man. I must get to know him better."
—Abraham Lincoln (whose instinct here is
the opposite of most, which is
why first impressions last)

In sales, especially, you rarely get a chance to make a second impression if the first is negative and, often, if it's simply not impressive or one that sets you apart from your competition in some way. First impressions take into account everything that represents your company, including and especially you. Personalities go a long way in terms of whether a relationship is established or not. Wouldn't the world be a wonderful place if we all thought like Abe Lincoln, giving people even more of a chance when we feel a certain discomfort—learning and going beyond the initial reaction to discover more about each other and ourselves? But unlike Lincoln, most people make snap judgments and stick with them. The old saying is true: *First impressions last.*

Your Office

If you have an office and you invite clients there, or if there is even a chance that a client would come to you for any reason, make sure that the image is one you want to project. Our surroundings represent us. Look around you—is your office saying what you want it to say? Even though you can reach into that swamp on your desk and retrieve exactly what you want, the image does not instill confidence in someone who plans to rely on you. If you're selling creative services, chances are that your surroundings demonstrate creativity. If you're selling fun, funky, colorful products, your office may look like a playroom. If your office does represent you, show a photograph of you and/or your staff or coworkers in that space in the "About Us" section of your Web site. If your surroundings are inviting, let people in through your Web site to see who you are and where your home base is.

Your Web Site

No matter what you do, more people by far will see your Web site than your physical office. When you meet people or send introductory material, they will usually look at your Web site if they have any interest at all. Your presentation begins with how you present yourself in person and online. If your Web site is out-of-date, looks old fashioned, or doesn't project the personality of your product or company, invest in an overhaul. Think of it as part of every presentation you make—because it is. Also, any additional information you can provide through your Web site—videos, downloads of brochures or other take-away material, an ongoing blog that would be of interest to clients and prospects—will help you to present the image that makes the sale.

Your Overall Web Presence

If you're online either personally or professionally or both at networking sites such as Facebook, LinkedIn, or Twitter, you can be light-hearted and friendly, but never lose the demeanor of a professional. Clients who Google you or link to you shouldn't find you flirting, insulting, or using foul language. Every phrase you utter on the Internet is public and represents you. Be careful to maintain a respectable presence—both offline *and* online. Any presentation you make will be affected by how you present yourself. If people have preconceived notions from Googling you before the presentation, let them be good ones!

Your Web presence should include a good photograph of you. Even in this highly technological world, and even though we often work with people whom we'll never actually meet, we all like to put a face to a voice or a name. Letting people see who you are is a good first step toward building trust. Use a good, close-up professional photograph. If you have a great picture of you in sunglasses that you think really expresses who you are, by all means use it as a secondary photograph. But use a primary photograph that shows your eyes. We still like to have a sense that we can look someone in the eye and may subliminally feel a lack of trust when we can't see someone's eyes. We can even get that feeling from a photograph, especially if it's someone we haven't met yet and that's the only image we see.

On Paper

In the megamarketing mania of the Internet, paper almost seems obsolete. However, your paper brochures and take-aways are still essential to your initial presentation of yourself and your company. Don't skimp on these because the information is available online. You want to leave a prospect with something tangible, attractive, and professional that speaks for you. Consider also making paper promotion available online through your Web site as a downloadable .pdf file. Beyond promotional items, the paper take-aways that you bring into a sales presentation are essential to reminding prospects of your main points and giving them something to hand off to others in the decision-making process. In this cyber world, don't forget the importance of your image on paper.

Why Choose You?

What makes you or your product or service unique? How do you target your presentation? Think about what makes your offering unique generally, but then think specifically about the potential appeal to each client before making your presentation. Your appeal is not how wonderful you are, but how wonderful you can make your clients appear, feel, or be—or how much you can affect that client's bottom line. Everything good about you comes back to them. Remember *WIIFM*—your client's first and foremost question before listening to your presentation and investing in your product or service—*"What's in it for me?"*

And again, remember that people are very often buying more than a product or service—they're buying a relationship with your company and with *you*. Sure, consumers calculate price, service, dependability, a good track record, and a host of other concerns, but we all know that personality is often the deciding factor. Prospects will be more likely to choose you when you inspire them and earn their trust. Inspire confidence, show enthusiasm, and let your personality shine through! Prospects who find you likeable, knowledgeable, and trustworthy will be most likely to become your clients.

Part Two

The Presentation

Chapter 3

The First Step

"Sometimes I wonder if voice mail was invented to ruin salespeople's lives."

—Steve Kaplan

Whether dealing with individuals or companies large or small, we have more ways than ever to make initial contact. Don't be so focused on your marketing plan that you forget how many possible avenues can lead to the same place. Try anything—networking events, Web networks, mailings, calls, advertising—but never forget that anyone you talk to might suddenly be an important resource. You might work out with someone side-by-side every week for a long time before you discover that you have mutual business interests. Be open, and pay attention. A salesperson recently told me about an executive he met through networking events. They never did business together but were always friendly at events. The executive brought his son to events over the years, who also enjoyed fun interactions with the salesperson. Twenty years later, the son entered the business world and became a customer and a strong source for referrals! Maintain friendly relationships, even if they don't seem to have an immediate result. You never know what may happen in the future.

Cold Calls

Sales-Success Mindsets

■ Cold calling, for many, is the most difficult aspect of sales.

■ You have to make fast friends, so the best openings are often the ones that make people smile and also get quickly to the point, letting them know that you realize they're busy but that you might have something of interest.

■ If you're cold calling, prepare an opening statement, but be comfortable with it; your opening lines shouldn't sound as though you're reading or as if you're reciting words rather than speaking to the person on the other end.

■ Rather than reading from a script, open a dialogue. Scripts sound robotic and create an instant disconnect with many prospects who might be responsive to a more genuine-sounding introduction.

■ If you hear a news event that is of interest to the prospect and leads into what you're offering, you might catch a prospect's attention by leading with that information.

■ Many sales professionals advise that, unless your phone number is set to "Private," you should avoid leaving voice mail. If you're unknown, you will be less likely to receive a callback than to capture someone's attention on the phone. (If, on the other hand, your name shows up repeatedly on a caller ID with no voice mail, you risk being seen as a pest, even if you haven't left a message yet or have left only one.)

➡

- Other sales professionals believe that voice mail is the cold caller's best friend. It gives you an opportunity to leave pertinent information uninterrupted, and if you get a callback, you know that someone is (1) actually interested and (2) calling when he or she actually has a few minutes to listen. (Whether or not you agree, it's the age of caller ID, so embrace the positive and come up with a tight, strong message.)

- Expect rejection, and don't take it personally.

- Each *no* is just part of the journey to your next *yes*.

- Cold calling is a numbers game. If the numbers aren't working in favor of you, sit back and reevaluate your approach. Maybe your techniques and phrases can be refined, but maybe you would benefit from shifting your strategy to one that invests more energy into other marketing and networking efforts. Change is the only true constant. Finding and refining what works for you should be an ongoing process.

Phrases

- "I wonder if you could help me. I have a product/service that is designed to increase Internet security. Who would be the best person for me to speak with?"

- "Thank you for taking my call. I'm with a local firm that specializes in creating low-cost promotional programs that draw big attention to small companies."

- "I'm offering a free marketing consultation to local businesses. Can you tell me who I should speak with about that?"

- "I'm calling from ABC Wholesalers. Do you know that you can save between 40 and 60 percent on household products?"

- "I'm calling homes/businesses in your area because of the rash of break-ins lately. We offer the most reliable security systems on the market. I'd be happy to come to your home to give you a free estimate."

- "From whom do you currently buy comparable products/services? Are you happy with that relationship? In what way could that product/service/company better meet your needs?"

- "I understand you're in a rush. What might be a good time for me to call back?"

- "I think you'd be interested to see what we've done for XYZ Corp.'s bottom line. When could we meet?"

- "My company has some innovative ideas for marketing that have been opening up new avenues for companies in your industry. I'd love to show you what we've been doing to see what results we can generate for you. Would you have any time next week to see what we have to offer?"

- "We have a no-lose offer. If you're not happy, we provide a full refund."

- "This risk-free offer allows you to try our product/service with no money down."

- "I understand how busy you are. This product/service is designed to save you time. If I can have just 20 minutes of your time, I can show you how you can start saving time and money right away."

- "I realize you're busy, but if I have something that could increase your sales/lower your taxes/drive in more business/increase your visibility/revitalize your Web presence—would you have 20 minutes to take a look?"

- "Let me show you how you can cut taxes by 20 percent/increase profits/increase business substantially by entering new markets."

- "I understand that you have limited time. Would increasing your bottom line by 20 percent be worth your time?"

- "I understand that you're happy with your broker/agent/representative, but have you seen what another broker/agent/representative might be able to offer?"

Sales-Success Mindsets

- Create as many opportunities as possible to encourage prospective clients to reach out to you for information. Once someone's reached out to you, you usually can expect a warmer reception than you would with a cold call.

- Don't be put off by cold receptions to warm calls. People may forget that they reached out, and some people second-guess having left their phone numbers. If someone was referred, that person may not be as open as the person who referred you thought he or she might be.

- Sometimes a cold reception once you've had an inquiry or introduction has nothing to do with you, your product or service, or the prospect's interest in learning more. Sometimes it's just a bad day or a bad time.

- If you're following up from an e-mail inquiry, be sure to make that clear upfront.

- A call from a company that is being responsive to inquiries will be far more welcome than a cold call.

- A reference helps your prospect feel comfortable putting his or her guard down—at least somewhat. Drop the name before your prospect drops your call. If you sound like just another random sales call to a busy, frustrated prospect, you may lose your chance to show that you have more of a connection.

- Showing that you have been given the lead by someone who knows and trusts you—probably someone with whom you've worked—builds trust. However, if you say that someone encouraged you to call and that isn't what happened, you completely undermine your credibility.

- Don't just remind people of your company name (unless the name itself is descriptive of what you do, e.g., Harding Realty). People might remember you and your conversation with a little more prompting, but few people will remember offhand the names and company names of everyone they meet.

- If you have a conversation with someone who might be interested in what you offer, jot down notes immediately afterward, and look back at those notes before you make a call. Have relevant information at hand to jog your prospect's memory of what you discussed.

Phrases

- "Hello. I'm following up from your e-mail inquiry to [company name]."

- "Thank you for requesting a call from XYZ Corporation. I have a note here that you requested additional information and had some questions. If you have just a few moments now, I can assist you with that."

- "Jack Frost suggested that I call you. He's been so happy with the results he's seen from working with us at JB and Sons that he suggested I call you to explore how we can generate those results for you."

➡

- "I just spoke with Helen Farmer, who said that she forwarded some information about BBK's business services. She said that she had a sense that our services would be a perfect fit for your current needs."

- "When we spoke back in May, you suggested calling this week to schedule a meeting. I'm available next Wednesday or Thursday. What works best for you?"

- "I met your general manager, Randy, at a trade show in Dallas last month. He said that you would be the one to speak with about purchasing decisions. I have some top-quality green products that I think your customers will love. What would be a good time to come by and show you what we have to offer?"

- "Hi Jim, this is Sarah Parker. We met at last month's Chamber event. You said that you'd like to hear more about our catering services, so I'm just following up. How are you?"

- "Tell me some good news. Since we met at the conference, you signed six deals, and you need larger offices/upgraded equipment/staffing solutions/financing, right?"

- "I enjoyed talking with you at the trade show, and I'm really looking forward to continuing our discussion. What would be a good time for you?"

- "Thank you for filling out our survey. I understand your situation, and I believe we can help you with that. When can we get together to discuss what we can do?"

- "Thank you for writing. I'm sorry for the trouble you had with our Web site. We're working on that now, but I can take your information personally to ensure that you have a quick reply and an accurate estimate. Do you have a few minutes now?"

■ "Hi. We haven't met yet, but I'm also a member of the ABC, and I'm reaching out to other members with a special offer."

Closing the Cold or Warm Call

Sales-Success Mindsets

- Be persistent. According to AllBusiness.com, "Eighty percent of new sales are made after the fifth contact, but the majority of salespeople give up after the second call."

- Don't panic if the call is ending and you don't have the appointment. You're building a relationship.

- It's more important to keep things friendly than to push so hard that you become perceived as a pest or as someone who is not considerate of the prospect's time.

- You may not get the appointment on the first call. Remember that you're building a relationship.

- Encourage but don't push so hard that your calls are no longer welcome.

- You might be more likely to set a brief, preliminary meeting than a long appointment for a full presentation. Use that opportunity to meet someone face-to-face. After that, you're more likely to be invited to offer your full presentation.

Phrases

- "Does this touch on issues that are of concern to you right now?"
- "Is this something you'd like to explore further?"
- "Would you like me to send you something about how our service can help you? I'll be happy to send it at no

cost or obligation. My number is on the literature. Please call after you've had a chance to look it over, or I'll call you in a few weeks."

- "I'll be in your area on Wednesday. Would you have 15 minutes to spare if I came by at 10 a.m.?"

- "What would be a good time for me to stop by briefly to introduce myself and leave you with a sample?"

- "The presentation takes about 20 minutes, but if I could have an hour, we would have plenty of time in case anyone has questions or would like to discuss things further."

- "Would Tuesday at 11 a.m. be a good time to meet?"

- "I can drop by your office at 2:30 today to discuss this further. Or would tomorrow morning be better for you?"

Hot Calls

Sales-Success Mindsets

■ It's easier in a hot call than a warm or cold call to move from conversation to suggesting a time to meet.

■ Hot calls allow you to be more familiar and more natural.

■ The more you know someone, the easier it is to have a natural conversation.

■ Don't oversell existing clients, but if you have something else they need, you have the advantage of having already established trust.

■ If you've spoken before, remember details of the conversation. Asking how the trip was or how the big meeting went shows interest and helps to establish a relationship. Be careful not to take note of every little thing and run down the list asking about them. It's obvious what you're doing and doesn't lead to a pleasant, relaxed conversation. Just recalling a few points or asking one or two polite questions will show your interest.

■ If someone shows some interest in a strictly social situation, don't give your whole presentation. No one wants to feel cornered by a salesperson—and people will easily feel cornered even if they asked the initial question.

Phrases

■ "Hi. This is Jackie Ringwald. We were talking at Hiroko's party last weekend."

- "Hi. This is Trish Fargo. My friend/colleague/client Joel Bergman said that you'd be expecting my call."

- "We've been corresponding so long online that I feel like I know you. I'll be traveling to the San Francisco area later this month if you'd like to meet in person."

- "Hi Jack. How are you? Have you been enjoying our service? We have a few new features that I think will enhance your experience. What would be a good time for me to give you a tour of our new options?"

- "Thanks for reaching out. Let's schedule a time when we can sit down together so that I can answer your questions and show you what we have to offer?"

- "Hi Julia. Great news! We have an update that makes our system even more customizable for you. What would be the best day for me to come by?"

- "I'm taking a trip to your area next month. We've been corresponding for a while now online about business possibilities. Would you like to continue this conversation in person?"

- "Lena Prabhu asked me to give you a call to see what we can do to help your business grow. I'd be happy to meet with you. What does your schedule look like?"

- "We've been friends a long time. I'd be glad to help in any way I can. When can we sit down to talk about this?"

- "I'm glad my advice on the message boards was helpful. Thanks for reaching out to find out more about my consulting services. When would you like to sit down and talk about your needs and how I might be able to help you?"

- "It was great to hear from you! How have you been? What can I do for you?"

- "Hi. Remember me? We met at the Gazette's fund-raising event, and you said that I should give you a call this week to discuss your marketing plan."

- "Hi, Jack. How are you? How have our solutions been working for you? I have some new options that will lower your cost and offer even greater benefits. What would be a good day for me to come by and show you how you can take advantage of them?"

- "How are things going? Have you had a chance to try the upgrade demo I sent?"

- "The industry's been going through some changes, and we've been offering deals and incentives to new clients. I appreciate your business, and I think at this point that we can reevaluate your plan to see how we can revise it to save you money."

Networking in Person

Sales-Success Mindsets

■ Join associations, and go to networking events, conferences, and trade shows. Build relationships. Even if you don't see results right away, when people get to know you and like you, they'll think of you when a need arises for your product or service. Anyone who likes you and understands what you do will be a possible source for referrals.

■ Don't cut off associations because they don't "pay off." All relationships eventually can bring business. Everyone is either a potential prospect or someone who might connect you with potential prospects.

■ Reach out to competitors. Your competitor is not your enemy and might even become a trusted friend, confidant, and someone with whom you might work or share referrals when one of you offers something or has availability that the other does not.

■ When someone has paid for a booth at a trade show, don't walk in talking about what you do. Look at what they offer, show an interest, open a conversation, and then you can begin to talk about what you do and see whether you can arrange to talk more about what you might do for his or her business.

■ At events, don't wait for others to approach you. You'll look and feel awkward if you spend too long without engaging anyone.

- Some yes/no questions are fine, but try to think of open questions to start conversations. Yes/no questions won't easily start a conversation rolling.

- If someone's sporting a tie that shows his love of baseball or wearing a pink ribbon pin that shows her support of breast cancer research, comment on it, and ask questions. They'll obviously have passion for these subjects; they've gone out of their way to wear these conversation starters.

- Put people at ease by being relaxed, making them laugh, and listening to their stories.

- Introduce people, and make connections. If you're the catalyst for getting someone a great job, that person more than likely will be eager to do the same for you. Don't do it hoping for a return; just know that when you put out positive energy and help others, good things generally come back your way.

- If people show interest in what you have to offer in a social situation, answer questions briefly but succinctly. Pass along your card, and take theirs. Sometimes people will want to engage in a longer conversation; read signals carefully. Most often it's best to give enough to pique their interest and suggest following up at a better time.

- Be careful to keep social situations sociable, even if someone at a party shows genuine interest in your industry, your company, what you do, or how you got there, and how and why the other person is so interested in learning more. Don't forge into a lengthy conversation or go for the close. Relax. If you're pushy, you'll be remembered that way and be quickly brushed off; if you're relaxed, your interesting conversation and your expertise will be remembered when you have a more appropriate opportunity to reach out and speak more in depth.

Phrases

- "Great to see you again!"

- "I haven't seen you before. Are you new to the organization? What do you think of it so far?"

- "What an interesting business you're in! Can I have your card? Here, let me give you mine, too. I sell commercial real estate."

- "Sounds like you're in an interesting business. Tell me about it."

- "You sell insurance, also? Great to meet you! Have you made good connections through this organization?"

- "Yes, I've heard of your company. I'd like to hear more about what you do. I also think we might have some common interests. My company arranges special engagements for motivational speakers."

- "We really should get together. Would you like to drop by my office sometime?"

- "What a terrific brochure! Very interesting. I'd like to send you some of our materials so that you can see more about the services we've been talking about. Would it be alright if I send that along?"

- "You're looking for an accountant? I was just talking to an accountant friend of mine. Let me introduce you."

- "Thank you for the referrals! I'll keep an ear out for people who would be interested in what you do, too!"

- "I'm glad I was able to help make that connection for you. I think that you two are a great match! If there's ever anything I can do for you, just give me a call."

- "I don't know if we'll ever have occasion to work together, but I always enjoy seeing you!"

- "We've been talking a while now at these events, and I really think that we could have some interesting solutions for you that are right in line with where you're heading. Can we schedule a time when I can share these ideas with you?"

- "You've always got such interesting ideas. I'd love to hear more. I also think that we might have some common goals and things we might do together. Would you like to have lunch sometime?"

- "It's always great to see you! If you're ever interested in talking about insurance/security/training/merchandising, I'd be happy to come by at your convenience. Do you have my card?"

- "I hear that you're a chiropractor, and I may need your services. I also hear that you're looking for a new home. I'm in real estate. Maybe we can help each other."

- "What an interesting pin. Does it have any special significance?"

- "I love your golf tie! I'm new in the area. What's your favorite course around here?"
- "I recognize you! We're linked through a networking site. I've noticed your funny updates. I feel like I know you!"

Sales-Success Mindsets

■ If you don't have a presence in professional online networking sites, do it! You'll meet people, find referrals, and get your name out there.

■ Keep your online business presence professional. Beyond professional and networking sites, make sure that any personal site, photos, or social networking site doesn't contain comments, photos, or any content that could be offensive or jeopardize your image as a professional.

■ Expand your Web presence, but be cautious of joining too many sites that will require you to keep up with them.

■ Always stick to the guidelines of bulletin boards and networking sites.

■ If a board is for discussion only and not marketing, stick to the discussion. Your best marketing here is to let people see who you are and what you have to add to the discussion. Provide accurate, up-to-date information on your profile. Once they get to know you through the site and respect your comments, they'll know how to find you.

■ Be friendly. Leave positive comments in response to postings you appreciate.

■ Web sites that are interesting, informative, or funny or offer free downloads are great conversation openers for cold calls or introductory e-mails. If the site offers

41

something free that you were able to use, begin by showing your appreciation.

- Social networking sites can be as lucrative as business networking sites. Again, it's okay to let people know who you are and to be informal, but always present yourself in a way that you would be comfortable having your top clients or prospects see—because they might. In fact, the odds are strong that they will.

- Creating a blog and responding to comments is a great way to show what you have to offer and to keep people coming to you to see what's new, but a newsletter or blog should offer some real information and insights and not just be a string of teasers. Let people see what you have to offer; make it enticing to subscribe to and forward to others, and your audience will continually expand.

- Never complain about a client or give too much information about any particular situation online. You never know who will see your posts. Also, no matter what the situation, you'll be the one to look bad in the end.

Phrases

- "I find your profile very interesting and would like to link with you."

- "Thank you for your comments. I appreciate your taking the time to put those ideas across."

- "Thanks for your advice. I'd be happy to return the favor. If you have any question that I can answer for you, please feel free to ask."

- "I'm happy to help, but I have limitations as to how helpful I can be without knowing your full situation. If you'd like to come in for a consultation, I can gain a better understanding of your situation."

- "Thanks for linking with me. If you'd like to chat—online or by phone—I think we'd have some interesting potentials for doing business together."

- "Thank you for making your booklets available for free downloading. I found the 'Nutrition Quick Facts' especially useful. I create informational videos and think we could create something that will be entertaining and informative and lead more people to your center. If that sounds interesting, please don't hesitate to write or call."

- "I agree with the comment made by Susan B. Thanks for stating it so clearly, Susan!"

- "Congratulations on the new job! Way to go!"

- "This discussion has taken a number of interesting turns and raised a lot of questions. I have some information that might be helpful."

- "I've enjoyed meeting you online. I was very interested to see the strong customer-feedback focus on your Web site. My company designs interactive feedback forums that might interest you. Please take a look and let me know whether you'd like to talk about what we can create for you."

- "It's been such a pleasure to correspond with you online, and we have some interesting business prospects between us. Would you like to meet for coffee next week?"

Chapter 4

Preparation

"The will to win is worthless if you don't have the will to prepare."

—Thane Yost

It's the day of the presentation. You've overslept. You're rushing, panicked. You think that you've missed it. Suddenly, though, there you are. Your notes are in a jumble, and as you try to sort it out, you hear the whole room tittering, snickering, bursting into cruel howls of laughter. Yes, the notes are the least of your problems. You're naked. Mercifully, the alarm goes off, and it was all a bad dream. Unfortunately, this is the moment—as you have only an hour before you head out for the appointment—that you wonder whether maybe you haven't prepared enough!

Sales-Success Mindsets

- Visualize the appointment going smoothly, practice, and role-play. As with any skill, practice makes a big difference in your comfort, your performance, and your ultimate success.

- Anticipate questions, and ensure that you have the correct answers at hand.

- Think about past appointments that didn't go well. What didn't go well? What can you do differently? What objections caused the greatest problems—and how can you answer those objections to your prospect's satisfaction this time?

- Bring printed material. If your company doesn't have printed material that is often requested, prepare something that you can leave behind with the requested information. (Unless you're in business for yourself, ensure first that any printed material you intend to give out meets company standards.)

- Appearance matters! Are you dressed for success? You don't need expensive clothes to make a good impression, but wrinkles, spots, and frayed threads don't inspire confidence.

- Ensure being on time by preparing to leave early. This way you can minimize time lost to traffic or other unexpected delays.

- Let people know that you'll be in an appointment. If a matter needs to be attended to during that time, make sure that you speak to someone who can handle it for you. Part of preparing for an appointment is making sure that you don't have to answer your phone during that time. All your attention should be on your prospective customer.

- Consider your audience. Your presentation and even the material you bring may be different depending on your prospect. Imagine, before you go, being your prospect. What do you want to know? What will your concerns be? What information would sway you in favor of *this* company's product or service over another's? Customize your presentation as much as possible.

- Make a list of possible objections and the answers to them. Include the hard ones that you don't think you have answers to. Focus especially on those. Brainstorm concerns. Discuss with others in your company and industry how to find creative, honest solutions that address those concerns.

- List the benefits of your company, product, or service. Include subheadings of benefits for particular groups or individuals. Keep the list handy. Add to it over time. Be very comfortable and familiar with it.

- Research industry publications and associations.

- When pricing a large job for a large company, you can often find industry (and even company) spending guidelines online.

- When your prices vary, find out all you can about your prospect's budget and spending patterns.

Phrases

Ask yourself (or your direct reports):

- "Am I as prepared as I could be?"

- "Do I know my audience?"

- "Have I done my research?"

- "Have I thought through my key points?"

- "Do I have clear, helpful material to leave behind?"

- "Have I thought through possible objections and possible responses and solutions to each one?"

- "What can I offer that is more than the competition is offering?"

- "Am I thoroughly familiar with my product/service and how it compares with others on the market?"

- "How is my service or product useful to this client?"

- "What outcomes am I hoping for by the end of this presentation? (Another appointment, a meeting with a key decision maker, a signed contract?) What is the best closing line to encourage this action?"

- "Based on what I know about this client, what are the most important points for me to get across?"

- "What do I most want to learn about the client? What key questions can I ask before the presentation? What questions should I ask during the presentation?"

- "What interesting stories or analogies do I have that will capture this prospect's imagination?"

- "What learning experiences from past presentations can help me to strengthen this one?"

- "Do I look the part of someone who is successful and self-assured?"

- "What are my product's/service's greatest assets, and how do those align with what I perceive is most important to this prospect?"

- "Have I done my homework?"

- "Have I created an agenda so that people can follow along?"

- "Do I have visuals that enhance the presentation and make it more entertaining?"

Do You Know the Competition?

Sales-Success Mindsets

- If your competitor is publicly held, find its annual reports to the U.S. Securities and Exchange Commission. Among other information, you'll find sales volume, revenue increases, and market share.

- Don't insult or denigrate the competition.

- Know as much as you can about your competition. Even though you don't want to say anything negative about the competition in a presentation, knowing all you can will help you to know where you stand, strengthen your edge, and be ready to answer objections raised by prospects who have investigated their other options.

- Who are your strongest competitors? Look into articles and online resources to learn what you can about them.

- Following are some useful resources for finding data about your competitors: *Ward's Business Directory of U.S. Private and Public Companies, Dunn and Bradstreet Million Dollar Database,* and *Almanac of Business and Industrial Financial Ratios.*

- If you have something positive to say about the competition, that doesn't hurt your position. You can be respectful of the competition and still show why your company is a better choice and why your company's product or service is a better investment.

Phrases

Ask yourself (or your team members) these questions about the competition:

- "Who are my top two competitors?"
- "What do they offer, and how is it similar or dissimilar in the following areas?"

  "Price?"

  "Durability?"

  "Value?"

  "Name recognition?"

  "Customer service?"

  "Convenience?"

  "Ethics?"

  "Other?"

- "How long have they been in business?"
- "What do I know about the competition's reputation in the eyes of the average customer?"
- "In what areas am I at an advantage when measured against the competition?"
- "What is my biggest competitive edge?"

Preappointment Questions

Sales-Success Mindsets

- Find out who will be meeting with you in addition to the person with whom you originally set up the meeting.

- If you want to bring a colleague with you, ask prior to the appointment.

- If you have any special setup needs, ask prior to the appointment.

- Make your presentation setup easy on the prospect.

- Don't ever assume something will be in the room. If something is essential to your presentation, ask or— better yet—bring it.

- Prepare a clearly written proposal.

- Provide a detailed proposal and summary.

- Prepare for the unexpected. If the connection won't work, your PowerPoint presentation will be useless. Create the best visuals you can, but be prepared to present without them.

- If you request a flip chart and markers for your low-tech presentation, expect the markers to be dried out. Bring your own. Better still, bring your flip chart too.

- Have at least two sets of extra handouts. You might be told that you'll be meeting with three people and find five when you arrive.

- Call to confirm meeting and presentation times.

Phrases

Ask your prospect:

- "Do you have a flip chart?"

- "I have a PowerPoint presentation on an Apple computer. Are you set up for that?" (You may need to bring an adaptor.)

- "How many people will be attending?"

- "Could I trouble you to e-mail me a list of those who will be attending and their job titles/departments/roles on the team?"

- "Please invite anyone you think would be interested."

- "Do you have a preferred format for proposals?"

- "What information do you require?"

- "I'm preparing an agenda to target the presentation. Do you have any objectives that you'd like to be sure that I cover?"

- "If you have no objection, I'd like to bring a colleague with me."

- "I'd like to let you know what I'll be going over at the meeting so that you can tell me if there's anything else you'd like me to prepare or research before we meet."

- "Hello. This is Jack B from XYZ. I'm calling to confirm our appointment tomorrow in your Weston office at 10 a.m. I'm looking forward to meeting you."

Foot-in-the-Door Questions

Sales-Success Mindsets

■ Once you have a foot in the door and have begun to develop a trusted relationship, you often can start to ask questions that otherwise might be difficult to ask.

■ You might have an inside track to finding out what the company values most if it isn't clear from its public material. Is it cost, quality, service, or sustainability?

■ If your prospect has a preferred vendor list, find out how you can be considered for that list.

■ If a large company has a core-supplier process that leaves you out of the loop, find out what the company needs and how to go about meeting that need, but going after a big fish if you're used to working with smaller companies can become consuming. Be careful not to neglect smaller clients.

■ If a company needs a detailed cost analysis in a way that you've never provided before, ask pertinent questions, but don't expect handholding. You're the professional, so go learn what you need to learn, and come back confident with exactly what the company requires.

■ Any offer available to you that you can stress up front to minimize risk will help you to make the appointment and, ultimately, the sale. No one wants to lose money, time, or "face." Risk reduction puts people's minds at ease and reduces some common objections.

➡

- Other ways that you can reduce the fear of risk is to show your experience, credibility, testimonials, associations, credentials, and anything that tells your prospects that you have a history of quality and reliability.

- Always follow guidelines, but add your own flair.

Phrases

- "Do you have a procurement program for my industry?"

- "Do you have a procurement program for my demographic [e.g., women, minorities, small businesses]?"

- "Can you explain how companies are chosen for your preferred vendor list? What do you require from me? Can you tell me how companies are evaluated?"

- "I'd like to be considered for your preferred vendor list. Who runs the program? Would it be possible for me to meet with him/her?" (Standard process may be sending forms to you to fill out, but meeting the people who make this decision could make the difference.)

- "You would know who the best people would be to see the full presentation. Would you help me connect with them to schedule appointments?"

- "Are there any specific issues I should address?"

- "I sent you a link to my bio and the company's testimonials page so that you can see what we do. If you'd like, I can send you hard copies."

- "I'd like to show you a company bio so that you can see who we are. Should I e-mail that to you directly?"

- "I realize that your time is valuable. I'd love to show you more [or talk more in-depth about how this could be useful to you], but I realize that my 15 minutes are almost up. Can we schedule a time for me to show you more?"

- "I can see that you're in a hurry. May I call you to schedule a time to meet with you?"

- "Thank you for allowing me to come by. I hope that we can schedule an appointment where we might have a little more time. Do you have any time next week?"

- "I'm familiar with some of the problems you're having with insurance plans. I know that policy prices are going up between 20 and 25 percent each year. I have a solution for you."

When You've Been Referred

Sales-Success Mindsets

- If you've been referred by someone else, there are a number of questions that can give you a better idea of who your audience will be.

- If a friend or client referred you, don't ask that person an overwhelming number of questions. You never want someone to regret doing you a favor.

- You might want to choose just a few pointed questions that are appropriate to ask and will help you to better target your presentation for the audience.

- Offer something in return or at least a token of appreciation.

- A handwritten thank-you card is always appreciated.

- Referral fees are one way to keep referrals coming, and it's easy to come up with an amount or percentage that makes everyone feel good about it.

- If you do pay a referral fee, you can feel more comfortable in asking more questions to help you make the sale because the person referring you has some financial interest in your success.

- Most people will refer you just because they'd like to do something nice and connect people they think will benefit from one another. For the same reason, they might be comfortable with answering one or two questions if those questions are appropriate and will help.

➡

- Be very careful to ask only appropriate questions. Even if you go in completely cold, you'll be fine, and no information is worth risking a relationship.

Phrases

- "Thank you for referring me to Ringside Productions! Is there anything you can tell me about them that might be helpful for targeting my presentation?"

- "I appreciate the referral. You've given me a few names. Which would you think is the best one to speak with about what I'm offering?"

- "I have a few questions about the company you referred me to, but if you're not comfortable giving out certain information, I completely understand. I appreciate the referral."

- "I realize that each situation is unique, but do you have any sense of what they've offered for similar services in the past?"

- "I appreciate your referral! I've sent a gift certificate to thank you, but please let me know if there's anything I can do for you in return."

- "Thank you for referring the Bards. I'll do my best to see that they enjoy the same quality of service that you have."

- "I know you've worked with them before. Would you be comfortable giving me some sense of what their budget allows for this kind of service?"

- "I appreciate the referral and would be happy to give you a referral fee. In fact, if you have other potential clients for me, we can establish a set referral fee."

"Thank you for the referral. Would you mind sending an e-mail introduction to me with a link to my site? This way, when I call, it won't just sound like I'm dropping your name. I want these people to know that we know each other and have a good working relationship."

Chapter 5

Presentation Pointers

"I offer you an algorithm: Find out the age of the oldest person in your audience, and divide it by two. That's your optimal font size."

> —Guy Kawasaki (to anyone who doesn't
> want to follow his standard advice:
> no font smaller than 30 points)

Ideally, a prospect will give you one hour to make your presentation. The presentation should be a solid 20 minutes, with time for people shuffling in late, equipment hookups and glitches, and questions and discussion afterward. The most sage advice regarding PowerPoint is Guy Kawasaki's 10/20/30 rule: 10 slides, a 20-minute presentation, and a 30-point font. One of the biggest mistakes in PowerPoint presentations is that people use too many slides and try to cram too much information onto each one. You may need more than 10 slides, but if you try to follow Kawasaki's advice, you might find that you don't need as many slides as you thought. PowerPoint is a complement, not a script.

Sales-Success Mindsets

■ Don't sell. Offer opportunities. Educate. Listen to what matters most, and see how you can be part of helping, partnering, enhancing, or energizing your prospect's vision.

■ Don't be afraid to offer some free advice. Let prospects see you as an advisor who has something to offer.

■ Make suggestions without being critical.

■ Know your material, but you might find it helpful to have some bulleted notes to ensure that you cover the most important points. As long as you're only glancing from time to time and not reading, this should be perfectly acceptable.

■ Make careful notes regarding your prospect's requests and concerns.

■ Keep notes on items you are to research, and follow through with a separate sheet to ensure that you don't forget or miss following through on any detail.

■ Don't read from a speech. If you bore people, you've lost them.

■ It may be helpful to have someone with you who might pick up on things you miss, see things from a different perspective, or even signal you when you're talking more than listening.

■ Stress your assets. If you're local, stress the value of being local. If you have a 24-hour call service, make sure that you stress that convenience.

- Whether you meet first with decision makers or with people who gather information for decision makers, treat everyone with equal respect.

- When speaking, warm drinks keep your vocal cords looser than cold drinks.

- You might be nervous before you get up to make your presentation—most people are. Remember that you're there to present interesting information and that you know your material. Focus on your prospect and your content, and you'll forget to worry about little things like your appearance or saying a few imperfect words in a long stream of perfectly targeted, perfectly fine phrases!

Phrases

- "Do you mind if I jot down a few notes? I want to be sure that I don't miss addressing or following up on anything that's important to you."

- "Please excuse my glancing at these notes. I want to be sure that I've covered everything that would help you in making your decision."

- *Privately, prior to the meeting or presentation*: "Would you mind if someone who's new on my team joins us for the meeting/presentation?"

- "Thank you for taking the time to meet with me and my partner, Mira. She has a lot to offer, and I think that it would help us serve you better if she's on the ground floor as we learn more about your needs and what we can do for you."

- "I have a preliminary suggestion…."
- "Here's what I noticed when I came in…."
- "I'd be happy to offer my opinion/thoughts/advice if you're interested."
- "Like you, we're a local business, and we care about the community."
- "Because we don't ever want our clients to be stuck if there is any problem with our system/product/service, we have a 24-hour call center where experienced agents are always on call to help."
- "I love what you're doing here. I can see how your vision is expanding, and I have a few ideas about how we can help you to achieve your goals."
- "I'm glad to be here to share this information with you!"

Getting Their Attention

Sales-Success Mindsets

- Show that you are familiar with the company. You won't get your audience's attention by talking about yourself and your company.

- Don't spend the first 10 minutes introducing yourself. You'll get your audience's attention by talking about what you know about them and how you can help them. If you start with them, you'll hold their attention.

- Once you have your audience's attention, they'll be more interested in knowing more about you and your company. Build trust by telling briefly about any associations you're in or awards you've received or what makes you unique.

- Show, don't tell. If you design Web sites, be ready to show samples; if you create brochures, have some in hand; if you are selling a product, bring your top-of-the-line item so that prospects can see, touch, and feel what it's like to use.

- Before you say how great your company is, show testimonials. Whether your testimonials are typed out or on video, people can relate to others who were seeking to achieve similar goals who found success through working with you. You can say that you have happy customers, but quote them—better yet, show them—and you will increase the impact of that statement immeasurably.

- If you show testimonials, make them brief! Don't waste time or make prospects feel that they're taking time out

➡

of their busy schedules to watch an infomercial for your company. Just include a few, brief statements for impact.

■ Your focus should be more on the prospect than you *or* your happy customers.

■ If you're doing great things in the world—showing you care or donating proceeds—make this part of your promotional material, and mention it early on, especially if you can see that your prospect is concerned and actively doing his or her part as well.

Phrases

■ "I'm here to focus on your needs."

■ "In looking back at your advertising campaigns, I noticed . . ."

■ "I'd like to share a brief video of some of our clients to give you an idea of how we've been able to help others in your field."

■ "Thank you for taking the time to speak with me last week. It's given me time to reflect on where you are and what we can do together."

■ "Here are some samples of our work. Of course, each job is unique, and we work to ensure that the final product has the look and feel of the company we're representing."

■ "I can run through a demo of our software, but would anyone like to give it a hands-on try? I think you'll like the feel of it and find that it's extremely user-friendly."

■ "I'd like to know more about your vision of how success will look."

- "I admire the work you did to raise money for children's funds. We have a scholarship fund that offers opportunities to teens who show great interest and promise in the arts."

- "We donate 15 percent of the proceeds from every sale to the environment/homeless shelters/animal rights."

- "Our new offices are designed to take full advantage of solar power."

- "All of our products are organic. In fact, we don't believe that the regulations for organic are as strict as they should be, so we hold our standards higher. We'd rather sacrifice a few dollars than our customers' health."

- "We care about reducing our carbon imprint/increasing environmental awareness/recycling our products/donating to those in need. I can see that you share our core beliefs about doing what we can to make a difference."

- "Most people in your industry are concerned about the economy/overseas markets/changes in the entertainment industry. I've been able to help my clients to make changes to meet these challenges and continue to prosper.

Putting Prospects at Ease

Sales-Success Mindsets

- Smile.
- Be yourself. People like people who are genuine.
- The more comfortable and relaxed you are, the more comfortable and relaxed others will be around you.
- Show confidence. Your confidence will tell prospects that they're spending their time wisely and will help to assure them that you have something of value to offer.
- If you make a mistake, laugh at yourself. We all make mistakes, and when we admit to being human, we're more personable and put others more at ease.
- Tell a joke or story that will lighten the mood and put the audience at ease. If they like you, they'll be much more inclined to listen to you!
- Never tell *any* joke or story that may offend *anyone*. If you're not sure whether a joke is a shade off-color, skip it.
- If you're not comfortable telling jokes, don't tell them. Better to be at ease than to look uneasy from trying too hard to look at ease.
- Be friendly and relaxed. Don't look at prospects as potential obstacles to the sale. Look at them as people you can help and allies who will help you by alerting you to possible roadblocks. They will only do so if they feel comfortable with you, and only then, when you know what stands in the way, can you remove those obstacles and make the sale.

➡

- If you arrive early or are waiting for others to come, make small talk. Don't just shuffle around nervously preparing or create an invisible wall as though you're a performer who doesn't fraternize with the audience.

Phrases

- *Your favorite joke . . .*
- *A story relevant to the situation or place . . .*
- "I'm so glad to meet you in person! Will Jim be here as well?"
- "The last time I was here in Chicago . . ."
- "Something funny happened on the way here. . . ."
- "I love your latest ad campaign. My four-year-old daughter sings the song all the time!"
- "I love this city! If I have one afternoon while I'm here to see something special, what would you recommend?"
- "I love your office/home! How long have you been here?"
- "I was just reading about your newest product/service."
- "How long have you been in this business? What first intrigued you about it?"
- "Do you enjoy living in New York?"

Sales-Success Mindsets

■ When writing your presentation, think about presenting yourself as an open book, not a mystery. A decision maker may be called out early, someone may lose interest, or long lead-ups simply will make people feel as though you're wasting their valuable time.

■ Although you don't want someone to leave early without having a clear understanding of what you have to offer, save something strong for the end. Your closing should always be strong.

■ Stay on point. Be extremely conscious of not wasting your prospect's time.

■ State before the presentation how much time you will need. Restate before you start how long you will take. Do not go beyond this time frame.

■ You will lose trust and credibility if you ask for 20 minutes and are still going strong at 30.

■ Watch your pace. Notice when you need to slow down.

■ Factor in time for questions, and encourage them.

■ Read your audience for clues, but don't overreact to them. If it seems as though you are losing people after 15 minutes, stop for a Q&A break.

■ Sometimes even the best plans require an on-the-spot revision. Be prepared to be flexible.

■ Acknowledge the value of your prospect's time.

Phrases

- "I'd like to have an hour of your time to show you what we can offer."

- "How much time will we have?"

- "This presentation will take approximately 20 minutes."

- "Let me begin by showing you the value we can bring to your organization."

- "I value your time, so I'll be careful to stay within the time frame we established. I'd be happy to stay as long as you'd like if you have additional questions or would like to see additional examples."

- "As you can see, I have other options that I'd be happy to show you, but I want to respect our time constraints, so I think I've put together a bundle that you'll be very happy with. If you feel that it's missing anything, please let me know, and we can refine the options."

- "I also have a short video, but I can see that we are running out of time. The video is about 10 minutes long. What do you think? Is it okay if we run slightly overtime?"

- "I'd like to come back to this, but I don't want to run out of time without addressing your questions. Does anyone have any questions or comments at this point?"

- "I realize that a few people have to leave early. Before I go on, do you have any questions?"

- "Well, we're running a bit early, but I think we've covered a lot, so I'll stop the presentation here, and we can use whatever time it takes for us to explore questions and discuss your thoughts."

- "Thank you for investing your time here today. I promise that it will be a worthwhile investment."
- "I appreciate your time. I know how valuable it is, so I'll be sure to spend our time here wisely."

Engaging the Prospect

Sales-Success Mindsets

- Engage your prospects as much as you can in the product or service.

- Talk *with* your prospects more than *to* them. Even in a presentation, do your best to engage your prospects.

- Questions engage.

- Getting your prospects to think engages them.

- If your prospects make jokes, play along. Always return to your point, but let them know that you can laugh along, even appreciate and incorporate their humor.

- If your prospects interject a story, thank them for sharing.

- Encouraging your prospects to finish your sentences brings them into the process, but never in ways that would make them feel like they could get the wrong answer or be embarrassed. If you use this technique, use it carefully for emphasis and with a touch of humor.

- Use people in the room for examples and scenarios, but be careful to choose people who seem open to being engaged in that way.

- Don't "call on" individuals for an answer or put anyone on the spot. It builds tension, not trust and comfort.

Phrases

- "What's your opinion on that?"
- "Can you see the benefit?"
- "Have you ever had an experience like that?"

- "Can you see how this would save you time?"

- "That's funny! Thanks for sharing that."

- "What do you think about that?"

- "Let's consider a scenario. Jim here walks into a showroom...."

- "Let's take Rhonda, for example...."

- "What would any of you do in that circumstance?"

- "Can anybody tell me ...?"

- "Does that statistic shock you?"

- "Does that concern you?"

- "How would you interpret these numbers?"

- "What do you think the results were?"

- "What do you think happened as a result?"

- "Did you see the study that was in the papers last week?"

- "You've now seen the studies. What conclusions do you draw from them?"

- "These are the answers people gave most often to this recent survey. What concerns do these responses raise for you?"

- "Before we get to the solution, I want to show you the full picture. Most people don't realize the full extent of the problem, so they don't know how to take action. You've seen the numbers. Do they concern you?"

- "It's clear that you want the best for your family, right?"

- "Of course, you want the best for your children."

Chapter 6

Focused Phrases for Any Presentation

"I went into a general store. They wouldn't let me buy anything specifically."

—Steven Wright

This chapter provides you with a general store of phrases. The core contains phrases specific to what you're selling. Of course, we can only reach a certain level of specificity here, but phrases focused on selling products will be, for the most part, different from phrases that you would use to sell services. Foundations for your personal store of general phrases begin with developing strong, convincing phrases for your product or service. Whether you're selling a product or service (or both), always remember to focus on your audience: What do they want? No one's really buying a product or service. They're buying the hope of a result, outcome, image, or feeling. If you're selling a product, you'll use some phrases based on features, and a service sale will use some phrases most effective for selling services, so these phrases are good foundations.

But remember that the essence of any sale is not what you're selling, but what the customer is hoping to gain. Think of benefits for every feature, and as always, accentuate the positive.

Selling Products

Sales-Success Mindsets

■ Show features, but focus always on benefits.

■ People don't buy products or services (e.g., a new copier, a seminar series, a yoga class) or features (e.g., a state-of-the-art sorter, books autographed by the presenter, a free yoga DVD) as much as they buy the *benefits* (e.g., convenience and a sharp image, feeling motivated and inspired, health and bliss). Focus on the benefits!

■ Stress the ease of your return/refund/replacement policies. These policies reduce risk for the prospect.

■ If you have a physical product that you can leave in the prospect's hands, always do so.

■ Stimulate the sense of touch—the sense of what it is to hold your product—and your prospect will be less likely to want to let go.

■ Come prepared with documents from sell sheets to product specs—anything that will leave the prospect with clearly stated terms to remember your most important points. These documents also will be useful to share with a decision maker who is not at the meeting.

■ Show the product, but don't turn the time you have for your presentation into product training.

Phrases

■ "This widget has more features than any other widget on the market."

- "You're right. This widget doesn't have more features than any other widget on the market, but it's the best-made widget and will outlast and outperform any other widget you will find."

- "The features this widget offers are in perfect alignment with the needs you're looking to meet."

- "Our software allows options for those who like to feel that work is play and for those who just want quiet functionality. I'm going to set it up both ways and let you try it. It's also easy to change options any time within the preferences panel."

- "Have you been enjoying the samples I sent last week?"

- "You're not just buying the product. You're buying access to our team of experts."

- "Our widget's greatest feature is compactness/price/quality/service/sustainability compatibility with other widgets."

- "It's clear that the environment is of utmost importance to your company. Our widgets are produced in an eco-friendly facility, and we encourage clients to recycle old widgets when it's time to replace them."

- "Our widgets have a 100 percent satisfaction guarantee. If you're not happy with our widgets, we'll take them back and refund your money with no questions asked."

- "How does it feel to hold/use this widget?"

- "Can you see yourself using this on a regular basis? What results would you expect if you used it every day?"

- "Now that you've held/tried/tested this widget, what do you like/enjoy/appreciate most about it?"

- "How would this widget change your daily schedule? Would it save you time? What would you do with that time?"
- "What features do you find most useful?"
- "How much time do you think it would save you to have a widget like this?"

Selling Services

Sales-Success Mindsets

- Don't focus on selling a service. Focus on meeting a need, and again, focus on benefits.

- Send ahead and leave behind anything you can that reflects your service.

- Video is a great way to connect and leave the feel of you, your company, and your service in the prospect's hands.

- Come prepared with documents such as process charts or return-on-investment (ROI) analyses—anything that will leave the prospect with clearly stated terms to remember your most important points. These documents also will be useful to share with a decision maker who is not at the meeting.

- Do your best to show tangible evidence of success. When selling intangible services, the more you can give that someone can see on paper or process as a strong, solid result, the more impact you will have.

- Will your service improve productivity? Reduce errors? Improve communication? Whatever claims you're making, put them in writing and include brief bullet points. In your presentation, run down the bullet points and offer a sentence or two about how each one will be achieved.

- When selling services, personality is especially important. Whether you're personally providing the service or not, when you don't have a physical object, more of the focus is on you.

- If you can, offer follow-up to ensure client satisfaction.

- Many prospects will fear salespeople promising concrete results and then using a scattershot approach without ensuring some client satisfaction. Understand that this is a natural fear, likely based on past experience.

- If you're selling a service that promotes you or someone in particular as the person who will be delivering the service, ensure that the prospect won't sign on and then have someone else show up. If you have someone else you trust and use as backup, put that up front. Let prospects know whether the choice will be theirs to either reschedule or use your backup person.

Phrases

- "I'm not here to '*sell* you.' I'm here to see how we can best help you achieve your vision and your goals. If we can't do that, I'd rather recommend someone who can than have you sign on and be unhappy."

- "We have an outstanding service department."

- "Our product/service/solution has a strong record of increasing sales/eliminating errors/improving productivity/boosting morale."

- "I've brought some process charts and ROI projections. I'd like to take a few moments to highlight some points that I think would be of special interest to you."

- "We follow through with you and your staff, checking in throughout the process to ensure success and make any necessary adjustments as we go."

- "After our training sessions, we conduct follow-up surveys. We also have a system in place to measure customer satisfaction."

- "We offer a free follow-up phone session."

- "Our representative will stop by once the system has been installed to ensure that things are running properly and to answer any questions."

- "We have an outstanding service department, but if you run into any problems getting through or having your needs met, you can still feel free to call me any time."

- "Either my partner or I will be working with you."

- "Your account will be handled by one of the people on the team whose profile you've seen. If we bring on anyone new, his or her experience and professionalism will meet the same high standards. If we assign anyone to you who isn't a good fit, please let us know. We want you to be happy."

- "I know that accessibility is of the utmost importance to my clients. You should always be able to reach someone who can help you, and I check my cell phone regularly. If you have any problems at all, you can always call me."

- "These seminars will motivate and inspire your employees!"

- "If you want a healthy, productive workforce, there is no greater investment you can make than a wellness program."

- "Our clients report employees not only taking fewer sick days but also having more energy and being more productive. They're also finding that they are better synergized as teams because they're learning to work as teams to inspire each other!"

Accentuate the Positive

Sales-Success Mindsets

- What's your company's strongest asset? Think of how this best applies to this particular prospect's needs.

- Even if it's a small company and you do it all, keep the marketing separate from sales. The marketing side wants to brag about the company. The sales side knows how to leverage success but also how to keep the focus on the prospect.

- What issues are of greatest importance to your client? Whether service, price, or particular measurable results, stress the benefit that your prospect cares most about.

- Have documents prepared that will provide answers to the most frequently asked questions or questions you imagine this prospect will ask.

- Leave behind anything you can that shows who you are and what you do—anything that you'd like perused or passed along after you go: brochures, cost-savings analysis, logistics sheets, price sheets, or more.

- Keep your presentation as simple as possible.

- If you care about the environment or any worthy cause, stress that—especially to an individual or a company that cares!

Phrases

- "When you call, you'll be greeted by a member of our client relations team. Each member is informed, knowledgeable, and committed to client care."

- "We provide flexible business solutions in environments where the only constant is change."

- "Our consulting team is composed of business and consulting experts who each possess cross-industry management experience."

- "Our team facilitates companywide solutions that provide a strong foundation for achieving organizational goals."

- "Our holistic approach addresses all aspects of business performance."

- "Confidentiality, obviously, is of great importance to you. Our clients' privacy is of utmost concern to us as well."

- "Because of the way our organization is structured, we can provide unparalleled, focused attention on each client."

- "You choose the functions, and we design a program that works for you. Your finished product is fully customized so that the training time for employees is minimal. We provide free training to all your employees and then free ongoing phone or chat-room tech support."

- "What sets us apart is our service. We have live people on the phones during business hours and an answering service after hours that will page a representative who can assist you."

- "We guarantee results."

- "We're the largest distributor of widgets in the Northeast."

- "We're new, which gives us the advantage of a fresh perspective."

- "Our customers rave about our service."

- "Our customers are drawn to us because of exclusivity/price/convenience."

The Competitive Edge

Sales-Success Mindsets

- Don't trash the competition.

- If a prospect mentions a particular strength of your competitor, acknowledge it and move on to discussing *your* strengths.

- Focus your sales presentation on the merits of your company's products or services.

- When faced with a choice, always take the high road; choose the positive perspective and be respectful of everyone—even the competition.

- If your competition is disreputable, they'll show themselves for what they are.

- While you wouldn't want to directly discredit anyone, it's a good practice to refer prospects to independent resources that rate companies, products, and services.

- If you have certifications or belong to organizations that support your credibility, point to those as significant resources for checking reliability and credibility.

- If you know of a Web site where people can register complaints about companies, it's okay to let prospects know about this resource and suggest that they check it.

- The competition might actually be a good ally for you and a source of referrals and shared businesses.

Phrases

- "No, I don't know much about that company. I can only speak to what we offer."

- "Yes, that's a good company. We've worked with them before. Our products and services are similar, but here's what I like about what we have to offer...."

- "Yes, I've heard about the prices they're offering. I'm not sure what they include in that. Here is a list of what we include, here's our guarantee, and here are the organizations that support us."

- "We do have a number of clients who used to work with them. I can't speak to what they offer, but here's what we give our clients."

- "I'm glad to hear you've looked into other options. The more informed you are, the more I think you'll appreciate what we have to offer."

- "They do have a good name in the industry, and their clients pay a premium for that name. If you compare our ingredients/components/results, you'll see that we offer products/services that are identical or nearly identical for a fraction of the cost."

- "Yes, I realize that that company charges less for a comparable product/service. But we stand behind our guarantees and offer personalized assistance that's rare in this industry."

- "Yes, that's a good company also, and what they do is similar, but I think we can offer better rates because of our size and affiliations."

- "I can't comment specifically on their policies or practices, but I would suggest that you check out the Web sites listed here before working with anyone, including us. You want to make sure that anyone with whom you work has these certifications. You also can see whether any complaints have been filed or if the company has been fined for any violations."

- "I'm not familiar with that company's products, but I would always suggest checking *Consumer Reports* before making any decisions. Our product, as you'll see, received top ratings."

- "We are certified, which means that we had to achieve certain standards. Even if you don't choose to work with us, I suggest that you make sure that anyone you work with has this certification."

- "There is a Web site that registers complaints about companies. It's a great consumer resource."

Chapter 7

Language, Style, and Creativity

"If opportunity doesn't knock, build a door."
—Milton Berle

How creative can you be in your presentations? Do you have a distinctive style? Do you "speak the customer's language"? Language matters. Don't use your jargon, but use theirs, and be cautious of word choice. A battery salesman told me about a woman who thought that her battery had died. She called him to replace it, but he looked under her hood and said, "It's not your battery. It's a terminal problem." She was devastated. "I need this car!" The difference between *terminal* and *connectivity* made all the difference. At least in this case it gave them a good laugh! Speaking of laughter, if you can make people smile, they're more likely to remember and be open to you and put down the wall of defenses that so many people raise when a salesperson enters the room. Have a good time with your prospects and your presentation—and with language, too. Smiles, creativity, and interesting language and images all make you—and your product or service—more memorable.

Winning Words and Phrases

Sales-Success Mindsets

- Use the prospect's name—and pronounce it correctly!
- Use positive language.
- Toss names in where you can, but be sure to keep it natural. People like to hear their names, and it makes them feel more connected to you if you use their names rather than seeming like someone who goes from company to company never really focusing on the individuals.
- Use positive, emotionally charged words.
- Don't be afraid to use the word *feel*. People very often buy based on emotion.
- Don't appeal to emotion alone. Logic has to agree, or the end result will be buyer's remorse and a likely return.
- Find out one of your prospect's interests, and see if you can incorporate it into the use of what you're trying to sell.
- Draw a picture with words, and put the prospect squarely and happily in the center of it.
- Minimize your use of *I, me,* and *we;* use more "you" language. People want to hear what you can do for them more than they want to hear all about you and your company.
- If you have a great, inspiring story about a client's success, then you have two great elements in one: a client's success story that points back to the benefits of working with your company and an interesting story

that evokes emotion and paints a vivid picture in the prospect's mind.

■ If you sell something that has a negative connotation, reframe it with other words. As long as your words accurately describe what you're selling, you're still telling the truth. (Thus the effort to rename prunes with the equally accurate name *dried plums*.) If you sell life insurance and you have lists of clients who've recently bought homes, talk about creating security with mortgage insurance because life insurance can be used for that purpose.

Phrases

■ "Polly, thank you for inviting me today."

■ "This is a great office, Chuck! What a wonderful view!"

■ "What an exciting new venture!"

■ "How does it make you feel to be behind the wheel?"

■ "I know your passion is wind sailing. This vacation package can really help you to explore some exciting destinations where you can experience that kind of freedom while you explore new, exotic places. Take a look at these photographs."

■ "Can you imagine yourself cooking a gourmet meal in this kitchen?"

■ "How do you feel about this?"

■ "Can you envision that this is your view when you come into the office in the morning? Does this seem like a view that would inspire you to go for that $10 million deal?"

➡

- "I can see the problem. That's a difficult one, but I'm sure that we can find you some creative solutions."

- "I can see that what you're looking for is a fairly complex solution. I love a challenge—and I believe that I can put together just what you're looking for!"

- "This system is not only extremely effective, but it's fun to use as well!"

- "Your family/wife/employees/customers will love this!"

- "Our most challenging request turned out to be our greatest success story! One of our clients . . ."

- "There are so many ways that furniture might be arranged in a room like this. What would you do with this room?"

Avoid These Imperfect Phrases

Sales-Success Mindsets

- Avoid clichés and worn-out phrases. They don't say anything, and they weaken your strong points.

- Don't say anything that isn't true.

- Talking too much about how honest you are will make you sound dishonest.

- Don't read exact phrases from your presentation slides.

- Don't insult the competition.

- If at all possible, avoid closing with a threat of an unreasonable change in price or availability if the contract is not signed immediately. Savvy clients will see through it and resent the attempt to manipulate as opposed to simply showing what you offer and allowing them to make an intelligent, carefully weighed decision.

- Don't talk about your commission or how the sale would benefit you.

- Don't complain about your company.

- Whatever you say, keep it clean! Foul language and dirty jokes will, without a doubt, cost you sales.

Phrases *to Avoid*

- "To tell you the truth . . ."
- "A child can do it."
- "This is truly the greatest thing since sliced bread."
- "Would I lie to you?"

- "I wouldn't lie to you!"
- "Today only . . ."
- "Just for you . . ."
- "Because I like you, I'm going to make you this special offer."
- "Excellence is our motto."
- "Service is our motto."
- "Honesty is our motto."
- "I'm going to advise you as I would if you were my own family."
- "The competition would say anything, but I'll tell you the truth!"
- "If we close today, I'm eligible to win a prize from the company."
- "I realize you don't want the added insurance, but can I just add it for my commission, and we can cancel it later?"
- "You'll never find a better deal."
- "I'm not going to tell you how to run your business, but . . ."

Insider Language

Sales-Success Mindsets

- Be careful not to use acronyms and buzzwords that leave your audience out.

- If you choose to use acronyms or buzzwords, define them.

- If you have coined your own acronyms, introduce them by writing them out or showing them on a slide.

- If you want to become part of a company's culture, learn the language. What are *their* acronyms and buzzwords? Do they call departments by certain nicknames? If you want to become an insider, sound like one.

- Tread lightly with personal nicknames; only use them when invited to do so. You can slip into familiarity with the company, but that level of personal familiarity with prospects will seem inappropriate if you use it without invitation.

- Listen and learn by context where you can. If a unique term is tossed out in a meeting, ask what it means. (If it would slow things down necessarily, make a note to ask someone in the company later.)

- If something is mentioned during a meeting that sounds derogatory, make a note, and quietly ask a trusted insider. You don't want to become involved with gossip or petty arguments, but it might be helpful to know if different departments are at odds—especially if one is involved with the decision making. (Be friendly with both, but know you might need to put some additional energy into having a strong relationship with both instead of being seen as aligned with one or the other.)

Phrases

- "Let me just define a few terms before I go on. You might be familiar with them, but many people aren't, so I like to be sure that I define them up front just in case."

- "We created our own software to simplify cost analysis. We call it EASE—Electronic Analysis Software Engine."

- "I'm sorry. Maybe I should know that term, but I'm not familiar with it. Would you mind defining it for me?"

- "I thought I was familiar with that acronym, but in this context I'm wondering whether you're using it in a different way. Can you define it for me just so that I'm sure I know what you mean?"

- *Very privately:* "During the meeting, I had a sense that there might be some tension between departments. Since both are involved in this decision, is there anything you think would be helpful for me to know about or any suggestions you can make for my not stepping on any toes along the way?"

- "I notice that you have quite an extensive inside language! Would you mind giving me a quick company language lesson before I meet with the rest of the team?"

Metaphorically Speaking

Sales-Success Mindsets

■ Use metaphors, similes, and analogies if you can. They leave people with good, strong images.

■ What's the difference between a metaphor and a simile? Similes use the word *like* or *as* and metaphors are more direct, referring to one thing as another. Metaphor: "A million-dollar sale is a home run." Simile: "A million dollar sale is like a home run." In business, these terms are often confused, but it doesn't matter. A simile is like a metaphor—and as long as you get the idea about using images, it really doesn't matter which one you use or what you call it!

■ Tell stories. Again, you want to create a vivid picture of some kind, something that sets you apart.

■ It's okay to use a colleague's anecdote and say it happened to your colleague.

■ Don't use a famous anecdote and pretend that it's your own! Never risk your credibility.

■ Transport the prospect to a scene of happiness/success/ relaxation/pleasure/pride or accomplishment.

■ Don't worry if it takes a few minutes to explain a metaphor so that people can get their minds around it— a great metaphor will give them an image to which they can relate.

■ Metaphors simplify, make things visual (and a lot of people are visual thinkers), and often will bring a smile

➡

and make what you're saying—along with you and your particular product or service—memorable.

- People will repeat a great metaphor. People who hear a great metaphor often will say, "That's great! Where did you hear that?"

- Even if your metaphor is nothing spectacular and won't be repeated at dinner parties, it is going to create a visual image in the moment that will help to wrap your prospect's mind around your product or service in an immediate, relatable way.

Phrases

- "This may seem more complex than the others on the market, but it's simple to learn and offers much more control. Did you ever drive a stick shift? This offers that same kind of control. See how this other product's software makes choices for you? Now try ours. See how you control more of the options? Which one makes you feel more in charge?"

- "Our alarm system rings both at the police station and at our security station. We call immediately when an alarm goes off and send out a response team at the same time. Our response time, experience, training, and personalized response are equivalent to having your own personal security team."

- "We understand that finding the right company to work with is a huge decision. This will, hopefully, be a long-term commitment, and you want to know that you'll be happy. It's almost like going into a marriage. That's why our contract allows for stages and checking in before moving forward and increasing the levels of commitment. First, we'll get to know each other, and then we will enter into the engagement before we sign the long-term contract. By that time, we'll know how compatible our needs, methods, and personalities are, and we can discuss moving forward into a long-term contract. From there, I anticipate a long, happy marriage!"

- "One of our clients just told me that if service contracts were cars, ours would be a Bentley."

- "Each contact you make through this system is planting a seed. Some may take time to sprout, but within the first three months you'll be amazed by the number of prospects that bloom!"

- "We tailor solutions and provide seamless service."

- "Your Web site is your online home. You want to make it inviting. When people drop by, you want them to stay a while, look around, and get to know you."

- "We make our rentals so comfortable and take such care to have every convenience that visiting will feel like coming home—but to a home that has a Jacuzzi overlooking the ocean!"

- "When we're catering your affair, you help us in the planning process so that we know how to create the day as you envision it. On that day, you're royalty. You don't think about anything. The food, the entertainment, the events will all unfold as you wish. All you need to do is receive your guests and enjoy

➡

yourself, and we'll make sure that everything is to your liking. When we say we give clients the royal treatment, we mean it!"

■ "The speakers we can arrange for the event are outstanding and will inspire your team. They're so well known and energetic that they're received with the same enthusiasm as rock stars. We can also talk about scheduling sessions throughout the week where these speakers can offer more personal attention. Your team members will not only benefit in immediate, measurable ways from these seminars, but they'll also love you for providing backstage passes to meet and interact with their favorite performers!"

■ "I love jazz. In fact, I like what I do because it's as close as I can be to a jazz musician without having any musical talent! These days, my business is all about improvisation, innovation, and being in a creative flow. Some people see the ever-changing industry and the growing scope of client needs as a problem, but I enjoy the flow of it, the feel of always creating new and exciting outcomes through different collaborations. All clients have their own unique rhythms and arrangements and organizational instruments, and it's always interesting and exciting to see what kind of rhythm we can find together."

■ "We can't be surprised that the bubble burst. That's what bubbles do, and that's why we need to take a conservative strategy and stick with it. The next time we see a beautiful bubble, let's not forget everything we

➡

learned about the nature of bubbles back when we were two years old!"

- "I think we've got a strong foundation to build something great!"
- "We operate behind the scenes. Our job is to make things run smoothly, but it's always your show!"

Chapter 8

Always Be Listening!

"What people really need is a good listening to."
—Mary Lou Casey

"ABC" has become a popular sales mantra that reminds salespeople to "Always Be Closing." Even more important is "ABL"—"Always Be Listening!" Prepare, anticipate, practice, and visualize. But then, when you walk into the room, be ready for anything! Listening is the most important skill for any salesperson to master. You can only meet the prospect's needs if you listen and understand what those needs are. Beyond listening, you have to show that you're listening and confirm that you heard correctly and understand. People will tell you what they want or need, but sometimes you need more information. In sales, part of being a good listener is also eliciting more information when necessary by asking good questions—then listening to the answers. Prepare, learn, and practice all you can—but don't forget to *always be listening*.

Listen for Success

Sales-Success Mindsets

- Most salespeople focus more on speaking than on listening; a great salesperson does the reverse.

- One of the most common mistakes salespeople make is talking too much.

- You learn more about what your prospect wants by listening than you do by speaking.

- You can't hear objections if you're speaking.

- Being a great speaker will only take you so far. People are most interested in what you say when it relates to them—and that only comes from listening.

- It's easy to fill the silence with sound because you're nervous or you start to assume what the prospect might be wondering about. Don't assume. Allow silences so that what you've said can be processed and prospects can formulate their own questions.

- Don't answer what you think your prospects are thinking! Allow them to formulate their thoughts so that you can answer their *real* questions.

- During your presentation, don't think that the more words you cram in per minute, the more your prospects will hear. Speak slowly, coherently, and deliberately.

- Pause!

- Selling past the close is a common error in sales. Put out your best—then stop talking and listen.

- Encourage people to talk about themselves, and show an interest.
- Be sure to get your important points across, but overall, try to let the prospect speak more than you do.

Phrases

- "Can you tell me more about exactly what you're looking for?"
- "What would the ideal package include for you?"
- "Is there anything else you'd like me to know about your company needs?"
- "What are the three features/services/benefits that are most important to you?"
- "Before I continue, do you have anything you'd like to ask or add?"
- "I realize that your situation is unique, and I've tried to understand the complexities of it. Please feel free to interrupt if you think I'm off track."
- "I'm listening."
- "Yes. I see. Go on."
- "Please continue."
- "Can you tell me more about your company?"
- "Thank you for sharing that."
- "Your information/insights/questions have been extremely helpful."

- "I do have a lot of information to share, but I will be sure to leave time to listen to you. After all, this meeting is about how we can best serve/support you."
- "What I hear you saying is . . ."
- *Silence—the thoughtful pause and a time for listening.*

Ask Good Big-Picture Questions

Sales-Success Mindsets

■ Don't ask questions that you can easily find the answers to with some basic company research. Use that information to gear your presentation, and save your questions for information that's not found so easily.

■ In addition to seeking information, think about questions that are interesting and thought-provoking.

■ Don't waste anyone's time by asking questions with obvious answers.

■ Don't ask questions that are likely to have negative answers. In a bad economy or to a company in an industry that is especially struggling, don't ask casually, "How's business?"

■ Questions such as "Are you concerned about making the wrong choice?" are not only obvious, but they also focus on the negative, and you don't learn anything new by asking them.

■ Unless you're using them sparingly in a specific way to drive home a point, obvious questions are pointless and detract from your presentation. Prospects don't want to answer obvious questions; they want to hear about what results might be achieved.

■ Don't ask obvious yes/no questions such as "Do you want to increase sales?" Reframe that question in a way that is more useful, or simply tell how your product/service/solution helps to increase sales.

- Go prepared with questions, but also listen carefully and ask good questions based on what you hear. *Always be listening!*

- The best questions will come from researching and listening to your prospects. You can only ask good questions if you're paying attention!

- Once you ask a question, stop. Wait for the answer. Don't jump in and answer your own questions.

- Open questions are always helpful. Closed questions (requiring short, often yes/no answers) can also be helpful for gauging interest along the way.

Phrases

- "I saw on your Web site that your company redefined its goals in light of the economic conditions. I have ideas about how we can help you to reach and even exceed those goals, but first what do you hope to achieve by using our service/product/solution?"

- "I realize that many of your competitors are projecting fewer foreign sales because of the economy. Is that a concern for you as well?"

- "I realize that your industry has been changing dramatically. Looking forward, who would you say is your ideal customer?"

- "You've made it clear that you want to improve employee relations and retention. Have you surveyed employees to find out what's most important to them?"

- "What would you say are the three greatest benefits or perks you currently offer to your employees?"

- "You said that you're looking to create a new image. What are your thoughts so far? When you envision your new image, what do you see?"

- "What is the time frame you've set to achieve your goals?"

- "What obstacles are you facing?"

- "The economy is creating some tough obstacles for everyone. Your industry faces particular difficulties, too. Which obstacles are most difficult for you? Which ones do you feel are most important to overcome in the short run?"

- "We provide some saving options and safety nets. It would help me to know what you're doing now to save and invest in your family's future. Can you give me a snapshot of your current financial plan?"

- "If you had a wish list, what would you want to have happen?"

- "What would your best-case scenario look like?"

- "Where do you think this industry is going?"

- "What do you envision for the company's future?"

- "How can we help you help your clients through tough times?"

- "Before we discuss the changes you're looking to implement, can you tell me more about where you've been and what's prompting this shift?"

- "That was an interesting story. What's your perspective now, looking back?"

Ask Good Basic Questions

Sales-Success Mindsets

- Interesting questions show that you're paying individual attention and that you understand concepts larger than the piece of the puzzle that you're bringing to the table. But basic questions are equally—if not more—important.

- Basic questions also should not be ones with obvious answers, although sometimes you might think they are.

- Sticking to a list of basic questions allows you to remember to ask questions that will guide you to knowing exactly what your prospect needs or wants.

- Asking basic questions keeps you from making assumptions that might be easy to make because we tend to generalize once we've worked with people or businesses who appear to be in the same position.

- Sometimes basic questions help the prospect to clarify his or her wants and desires.

- Sometimes basic questions lead the prospect to envisioning the use of your product or service, which is a strong motivator for moving forward.

- Some basic questions help to ensure that you and the client are on the same page.

- Don't just ask questions—*listen to the answers!*

Phrases

- "Can you explain to me what your specific needs are?"

- "What is it you want to accomplish that our product/service can help you to achieve?"

- "I can hear how important that feature is to you. Can you tell me why?"

- "What would you hope to gain if you invest in our process/system/training?"

- "Can you see where this product/service would save you/your company/your department money?"

- "What I'm proposing seems like it would fit right in with your goals and mission. What do you think? Do you envision that this would be helpful?"

- "Could you tell me exactly what it is you're looking for and how you hope to use this product/service?"

- "What is your organization hoping to accomplish this year?"

- "What are your sales goals for the year?"

- "What are this department's long- and short-term goals?"

- "How can I help you meet your goals?"

- "What is your most important target market?"

- "How can I help you to solve that problem?"

- "What is your current financial plan? Are you happy with your advisor?"

- "What do you envision for your children's education? What plans do you have in place right now?"

- "What else would you like to know?"

- "What results do you imagine you would see from using this product/service?"

➡

- "Have you ever used a similar product/service before? What was your experience? What did you like/dislike?"
- "What other companies/products/solutions are you considering?"

Show that You're Listening

Sales-Success Mindsets

- Confirm that you understand one another.

- Summarize your understanding of what was discussed and/or agreed on. Then check your accuracy with the prospect.

- If you're wrong or corrected in any way, don't be defensive. Be grateful! You have cleared up something that might help you to close the deal when even the smallest misunderstanding might be a deal breaker.

- Be aware of and acknowledge your listening challenges. If you realize you've interrupted, don't assume that it wasn't noticed. Stop yourself. Apologize, and then listen.

- Be careful not to look disinterested.

- The best way to *show* that you're listening is by actually *listening*. You can look at how to display the demeanor of someone who is listening, or you can just listen and your posture will be one of a listener.

- *Listen.* Don't just wait for your turn to speak or think about what you will say next.

- If prospects casually mention things that are light and personal, show that you're paying attention by asking about them.

Phrases

- "What I think you're saying is . . ."

- "Do you mind if I just stop us here to clarify? I want to be sure that I understand you."

➡

- "I apologize. I think I misunderstood earlier. What I thought was, . . . but it sounds as though you're saying … Is that correct?"

- "Do you mind if we summarize the key points we discussed? That will help me make sure that I understand."

- "Thank you for correcting me!"

- "I'm so sorry I cut you off! Please continue."

- "I'm listening. Please go on."

- "That's interesting! Thank you for sharing that insight/information/story."

- "That was an interesting point you made about the difference you noticed in service providers when you moved from New York."

- "I like the analogy you drew. It's a very good way to illustrate what we do. I might use that in my presentations."

- "I'm sorry to hear that you were having so many problems in the past. I'm sure we can alleviate those problems and help you to move forward without those frustrations."

- "The last time I saw you, you were trying to get tickets for a sold-out show. Did you have any luck?"

- "How is your online course going?"

- "Tell me . . ."

Encourage Questions

Sales-Success Mindsets

- Questions are a good sign. They show interest.

- Anticipate questions, and have your answers ready.

- Always make the prospect feel comfortable asking questions, and stress that no question is too basic.

- Even if a question makes it appear that the prospect was not listening, have heart. If there were no interest, no question would have been asked. Sometimes it's a lot to take in new information; sometimes people's minds just wander, and it's nothing personal.

- Announce in the beginning that you will be open to questions throughout and/or at the end, or only invite them at the end.

- Even if you only invite questions at the end, if someone has one during the presentation, answer it without hesitation. Again, they're showing interest. Also, if they're not following, you may lose them.

- Let people know that if they have a burning question in the middle of your presentation, they should ask. You may say that you're coming to that point or will address it later, but sometimes it's something that could be answered or misunderstood easily.

- Unanswered questions can become distractions or lead to incorrect assumptions. Any question that helps you to keep people on track is worth the interruption.

Phrases

- "Do you have any questions?"

- "I'm glad you asked that question!"

- "I'd like to open up to questions at the end, but please feel free to ask questions along the way if something is unclear."

- "I'm sorry. I may not have been clear about that. Let me see if I can offer a better explanation."

- "Have I explained things to your satisfaction?"

- "I hate to drone on too long! Does anyone have any thoughts or questions at this point?"

- "There's no such thing as a bad question."

- "That was a great question! Did I answer it to your satisfaction?"

- "Thank you for asking."

- "Do you have any other questions?"

- "Have any burning questions been left unanswered?"

- "If you think of any questions after I go, please feel free to call, text, or e-mail me. I'm always happy to answer questions."

When You Don't Know the Answer

Sales-Success Mindsets

- You don't know everything. No one does.

- When you don't know the answer, don't fake it—and don't lie.

- You won't lose credibility by not knowing something, but you will lose credibility if you try to answer a question and you clearly don't know or give a wrong answer.

- If you don't know, find out.

- Find out in the moment if you can. If not, find out the answer as soon as possible.

- If the information can mean the difference between closing and not closing, do all you can to track down the answer before leaving. If you're that close, don't walk away. People get busy, and the priority will be higher for people while you're in front of them, whether in your office or in your prospect's office or home.

- Always be sure that you're checking reliable sources.

- If an answer from another department or outside source doesn't sound right to you, double-check with someone else. It won't matter that the mistake wasn't yours. You're the one responsible for finding and passing along correct information. In the end, it's your client—or not.

Phrases

- "I don't know, but let me make a call when we take a break."

- "I think I can find out right away and give us some clarity on that."

- "I'm afraid I don't know, but I'll find out and get right back to you."

- "What an interesting question. It's never come up before."

- "I'll have to find out as soon as I get to the office and get back to you."

- "I can see where that would be important to you. I'll find out."

- "Would you mind if I make a quick call to find that answer for you?"

- "That's an insightful question. No one's asked that before, and frankly, I'm not sure. I may not be able to find out until Monday. Can I call you with that answer as soon as I find out?"

- "I never thought about that as a potential problem. Now that you mention it, we should address it. I'll get back to you by the end of the day."

- "I think I can find that out for you pretty quickly. Do you mind if I go online and take a look?"

- "I know there's been some good research on that issue. I'll find that and get it right to you."

Chapter 9

Answering Objections and Closing the Sale

"Every sale has five basic obstacles: no need, no money, no hurry, no desire, no trust."

—Zig Ziglar

A n objection is not a rejection, but a concern—not a closed door, but an opportunity. Every objection a prospect voices offers a chance for you to clarify or to offer new information or perspectives. Don't fear objections; embrace them. Know they're coming, and be ready for the ones you've heard before or those you can anticipate that you might hear, and also be thankful for the opportunity to answer them. Few sales are achieved without an objection or two or many along the way. A sale could be lost because of a hidden or unspoken objection that might easily have been countered with information that would put the prospect's mind at ease. If you fear objections, you will risk not being prepared with good answers, and you also may actively avoid hearing objections by not listening carefully or asking questions that would bring them to the surface. A good answer to an objection could be the difference between making or losing the sale.

Hidden or Unclear Objections

Sales-Success Mindsets

- Address the elephant in the room.

- If you know that an issue is likely to be on the prospect's mind, ask a question to bring the discussion to the forefront, giving you a chance to address the issue.

- If you know the prospect is currently working with someone else and unsure about switching, ask what concerns might be associated with switching.

- If you answer an objection and the prospect seems satisfied but still hesitant, ask what other questions or concerns the prospect has.

- Don't be afraid to hear more objections. They'll have a much stronger hold if they're unspoken and you don't have the opportunity to respond to them.

- Even the prospect may not be clear about why he or she is objecting, but at least you can get all known objections out into the light, where you can examine and counter them.

- Brainstorm your own list of possible objections based on your product/service/solution, and as always, brainstorm new questions particular to each new client or presentation.

Phrases

- "I've tried to address your needs directly. If I missed anything, please let me know. I want to ensure that we understand and are meeting your needs."

- "What concerns do you have, if any, about changing vendors/service providers/outlets/suppliers?"

- "You seem excited about the results you can achieve if we go forward, and I'm not sure that I fully understand your concerns. Could you clarify so that I can best answer your questions? I want to be helpful in giving you all the information you need to make your decision."

- "Typically, I notice that when people say they want to think it over, there's a concern that hasn't been brought to the forefront. Are you sure that you don't have any other questions or concerns?"

- "I understand that you want some time to think about it. Do you have any questions or concerns that I might be able to address to help you make your decision?"

- "Is there anything else you'd like to know?"

- "What else is on your mind?"

- "Is there any other information that I can provide to help you make your decision?"

- "Is there anyone else who needs to see this presentation in order for you to feel comfortable about making this decision?"

- "I'm not sure whether I'm reading you correctly, but I have a feeling that something came up that changed your level of enthusiasm or comfort. If I said anything that caused concern for you, please let me know. I'm not always as clear as I'd like to be, and I want to make sure that I don't inadvertently give you any misinformation."

- "You mentioned earlier that you had to run this by your other partners. Would it be helpful for me to sit in and speak with them directly?"
- "What do you think? I'd like to have your honest reaction, so please don't feel the need to pull any punches."
- "Do you have any other questions?"
- "Is there anything else you'd like to tell me?"
- "What would I have to modify for this to become the ideal solution for you?"
- "If you'd rather not make a decision right now, I can offer you a risk-free one-month trial. Would you like me to set that up for you?"
- "If you could change one thing, what would it be?"
- "If you had one concern, what would it be?"
- "What's your main fear?"
- "What's stopping you from acting?"
- "If you had no fear, what would you do?"

Objections: General

Sales-Success Mindsets

- Write out each of the objections you commonly hear, objections that surprised you, and objections that you might have yourself—then write out answers to each one.

- If one of your shortcomings is pointed out, address it honestly, and then you can go back to stressing your strengths.

- If an objection is strong, you might be able to restate it as a more subtle question. If the prospect accepts your rephrasing, even if there's some validity to the objection that you can't answer, at least you've toned down any exaggerated quality.

- Be creative, if possible, when seeking solutions to objections.

- If someone objects to something that's standard policy, see if that policy can be bent. Not every policy is absolutely essential in every case, and prospects will appreciate the extra effort. And know, the best you can, how far you can push the limits of certain policies.

- Once you propose a solution, confirm that you have put the prospect's mind at ease. Don't assume that you've solved it and can move on. Always ask.

- Even if you think that you've explained something clearly, give the prospect the benefit of the doubt and say that maybe you should have explained it more carefully. If you say that you already explained that but you'll say it again, you're being defensive—and you'll make your prospect too defensive, in return, to listen carefully to you.

- Many prospects need to say *no* before they say *yes* so that they feel like savvy customers.
- Always offer new information or insights before coming back for another answer. If someone's saying no, you need to offer a valid reason for saying yes. Without that, it's unlikely that any amount of prodding or cajoling will change someone's mind.
- When no is the answer, do what you can with regard to price, extras, benefits, upgrades, or anything else that adds value.
- Restating benefits is less likely to change someone's mind than offering additional value or information.
- Don't try to close before you've created comfort and given relevant facts. Also, be sure that you've done all that you could with language, images, and touching on an emotional reason to buy.
- If you know the prospect has a certain level of discomfort or lacks fundamental information, you won't get the close, and you'll seem like you're hard selling if you start pushing early. You'll only increase the gap between your prospect and his or her comfort level.
- Put people at ease by assuring them that there is little for them to do. The easier you can make the process on potential clients, the more likely it is that they will buy.

Phrases

- "That's a good point."
- "Fair question. Here's the answer."
- "It sounds like durability is your biggest concern. Is that correct?"
- "I understand your concerns."
- "I know how you feel. For a long time, I felt the same way. Then I realized _____ and became a customer. Once I got beyond that doubt, I loved this product/service so much that I decided to work for the company."
- "You've said that you're hesitant to try something new. Can you help me understand why? Maybe there's a way that I can lower the risk factor for you to make you more comfortable about giving us a try."
- "Does that answer your concern?"
- "That's our policy, but I can see it's a concern for you. In this case, I'll see what I can do to have that waived. I'll speak with my supervisor/partner tomorrow morning and call as soon as I have an answer for you. Do you have any other concerns?"
- "I see. Is there any other concern that you would have?"
- "If I understand what you're saying, you're asking how durable this will be and how long you can expect it to last."
- "I understand your concern. That would be a concern for me, too. Let's see what creative solutions we can find."

➡

- "Just to confirm, you'd like to fill out the paperwork and be ready to go ahead once I confirm, in writing, that we can honor this special rate. Is that correct?"
- "I understand why you weren't interested based on the five-year contract. But, if I can reduce it to the two-year contract and lock you in to these rates, would that interest you?"
- "Don't worry about the process. We'll make this very easy for you."
- "I realize that it's a lot of paperwork, but we'll fill it in, and all we need you to do is check to ensure accuracy."

Objections as Opportunities

Sales-Success Mindsets

- Objections become opportunities when you know to expect them and you have good answers and clear perspectives that put the prospect's mind at ease.
- Be thankful for objections. They tell you exactly what you need to address to make the sale.
- When you've answered a big objection satisfactorily, go for the close!
- Many of these answers to objections could be paired with and/or used as your close.
- If you don't fear objections, you know the value of "No."
- Treat objections as requests for more information.
- Acknowledge good questions and valid concerns. Seek to overcome objections, but never minimize the fears or concerns behind them.
- Sometimes, as with any concern, just stating and discussing the objection dispels the strength of it in the prospect's mind.

Phrases

- "I understand why you would be cautious about that. I would, too. That's why we offer low-cost plans to ensure you investment."
- "The product couldn't possibly sell for less and maintain this level of quality. I'm sure that you could find something that would look similar, but would you really want to sacrifice quality and reliability?"

- "Why do you say that?"

- "What leads you to believe that?"

- "Can you tell me more about that concern?"

- "I understand your concern. In fact, that's what a lot of my current clients said when I first met them. But when I was able to show them how they could overcome that problem, they succeeded. Let me share some of their success stories with you and show you how we can create the same results for you."

- "Great question! In fact, that happened to one of my clients. Let me tell you how we solved that problem. About a year ago . . ."

- "Just to make sure that I'm clear, if _____ and _____ were not issues, you would be interested in moving forward?"

- "I can see why you're hesitant because time is a factor, but saving time is the very reason you might be interested in what I have to show you."

- "If I can do _____, will we have a deal?"

- "Yes, I can see why you'd ask about that. Our small-town operation was a concern raised by XYZ Corporation, which has become a very satisfied customer. In fact, they offer the strongest endorsement on our Web site."

- "I'm glad you raised that concern. I'm afraid I wasn't as clear as I could have been. Let me explain."

- "I understand your hesitation. Suppose that we eliminated that as a concern. Would you be interested?"

Sales-Success Mindsets

- Because price is such a common objection across the board, have as many answers prepared as possible to the price objection.

- Many of the phrases suggested earlier for other objections also will work well for price objections.

- Many people object to price even when price is not a difficulty or even an objection because even though they may see the value in your product or service, we've all been conditioned to negotiate.

- Be clear on the value. If you can show a monetary benefit and relate it to the price, be as specific as you can.

- Acknowledge and validate, as always, the concern. Understand that not everyone is playing the negotiation game or undervaluing your product or service. Those who have real financial concerns and are still talking to you might be eager to work with you if you can do anything to affect price or payment schedules.

- If you are more expensive than the competition, don't say that you're not. Address the issue of value and what makes your product or service worth more. Is it quality, service, unique design features, or the level of training and expertise of your staff?

- If you have awards, recommendations, or reviews that show why yours is worth more, show the prospect. In the end, people will want to know that they're getting value, and they like to know that someone else has tested or reviewed and approved of what you offer.

- When closing, understand the stress that is often associated with spending money. But know that your product has value and that people are still spending money where they feel there is good value.

- If price is a large sum, break it down into payments if you can, and discuss the payments more than the lump sum. Also, use the words *deposit* and *investment* more than *payments, price,* or *fee.*

- You might want to do the math for prospects to show that for the years and time they'll use an item, the cost is less than _____ per day or year.

Phrases

- "I realize that cost is a concern, but this will help to save you money within the first three months."

- "I can hear that cost is a concern, but what value would you place on the benefits we discussed?"

- "Yes. I know some of our competition is less expensive, but if we meet their price, we can't afford to offer the level of service that we feel is so important for our clients."

- "I understand your concern with the upfront cost. The benefit is that for an upfront cost of $_____, you will save $_____ over the course of the first six months. Most clients earn their money back and begin enjoying substantially increased profits within the first year."

- "Yes, I understand that it's a big investment. What results would make that investment pay off for you? Let's look again at the results we can project for you."

- "You're likely to use this for the next five years at least. That would bring the price to less than $_____ per year. Does that seem like a good value?"

- "This is something you'll have for a long time and ultimately can pass down to your children. For all those years and the value of having something of such high quality to pass down, does that seem like a fair price?"

- "Is this a product that you'll use maybe four times per week—three conservatively? This means that the cost comes to $_____ per week/month/use. Does that sound like a good value?"

- "How often do you go for massages right now? How much are you spending each month? How much would you save in six months if you invested in this healthcare solution today? How much would you save in one year?"

- "The old system is twice as time-consuming as the new system. The question to ask yourself, as you consider this investment, is: *What is my time worth?*"

- "The price reflects the benefits, serve, and overall value. It reflects the quality that went into the product and the professionalism with which we serve our customers. Where else would you find a better value for your dollar?"

- "How would you feel if you could take this home today with no money down and 0 percent interest for six months? Have you considered our financing options?"

➡

- "If you hesitate now because of price, you're likely to end up paying more down the line. The prices have already gone up, and there's speculation that they'll be going up again this summer."

- "I can let you know when we're running specials."

- "We just ran a special. Let me see what I can do to get that price for you."

- "You may spend multiple times this amount of money later fixing the problem you could have avoided by making this small investment now."

- "A few dollars spent now can save you hundreds more later."

Presentation Closing

Sales-Success Mindsets

- Create a powerful close to your presentation.

- Summarize your presentation, and then give a great closing line.

- If you have an especially powerful quote or statistic, save it for the end.

- Even if your presentation isn't filled with powerful language, summon power words, a great quote or story, or ear-catching statistics for your close.

- Bring contracts. Even if you typically require a few meetings, always be prepared to close.

- If you've done your job, closing may come naturally.

- Be strong in your presentation closing in both language and visuals.

Phrases

- "And I'll close with a brief statement that summarizes everything we've been saying here today."

- "You may be wondering whether anyone has really been helped by this product, so I'd like to close with a few testimonial statements. I know that I gave you some facts and figures, but these are real people with real stories and powerful results."

- "Thank you for taking the time to listen. I enjoyed speaking with you and hope that it's been helpful. Are there any questions?"

- "What percentage of people do you think will be affected by this? Some estimates suggest 85 percent. What percentage of people do you think take measurable action in this direction? On average right now, only 10 percent. Are you part of that 85 percent? Or are you part of the 10 percent who care? The more 10 percenters we have, the more we begin to grow that percentage and make a difference."

- "What if you could have all this with no money down? What if it only took you four hours per week to be successful? What would stop you from making this investment right now?"

- "I'll make this the last slide because I know we'll have a lot to discuss now that you've gotten the full picture of what our program has to offer."

- "Our shopping club saves consumers an average of 40 percent per year on household items. What would you do with that extra money? How do you benefit by paying an additional 40 percent for the same products?"

- "When was the last time you invested in yourself?"

- "Opportunities like this come and go and often leave us with regrets, so I'd like to close with an old saying: *"If* and *when* were planted, and *nothing* grew."

- "I'd like to close where I began, by putting back up the same statistics you saw when you came in. Knowing what this product/service can do, do you think that you can avoid being one of these statistics?"

- "I'm stopping early because I can see how many questions are brewing here. I'd rather take more time for discussion and to answer your specific questions than to overload you with information that may not be relevant. What questions can I answer for you?"

- "The future is up to you. What will you make of it?"

- "I'll close by putting up our service guarantee. We pride ourselves on the fact that this guarantee goes beyond most in this industry, so we want to ensure that you realize the level of protection you will have before making any commitment."

- "It's been my pleasure to share this information with you. Can I answer any questions?"

- "What does all this mean to you? I'd like to close this presentation by showing you how much a company your size/couple your ages/family of five can save over one year by using this plan."

Closing the Deal

Sales-Success Mindsets

- Objection responses may be your closing lines, or closing lines may immediately follow your responses to objections. As you're building your store of phrases for the close, read all the topics in the "Objections" and "Closing the Deal" sections.

- Don't worry about asking again for the close; just make sure that you give more explanation, information, or value before you do.

- Asking directly for the close is difficult—there can be some emotional discomfort to spending.

- Sometimes you need to be more aggressive in your closing if you're likely to be forgotten or swept up with the competition in the prospect's memory.

- Sometimes a soft sell is the most appropriate, respectful approach and will work well.

- If you've made a good impression and offered a good value for the money, you can call to follow up, and you'll be remembered.

- A close is a call to action. Suggest the next steps.

- Sometimes you can't lower the price, but you can offer some extras that raise the value.

- Even when it's right there in front of you, and the prospect is clearly interested and eager to move forward, you usually will have to ask for the close. You can lose a sale by waiting for the prospect to say something as simple as "Let's do it" or "What's next?"

- Closing, even after a great presentation, doesn't always come naturally.
- Closing is an unnatural process that you've got to practice and make as natural as you can.

Phrases

- "I realize that you were going to make your decision by today. Do you need more information from me?"
- "Do you have any additional questions or concerns?"
- "I realize that you're not in a hurry, but if you truly do love it and it will make you and your family happy now, why wait?"
- "Let's fill out the paperwork so that we can ship your product/schedule your service/make your reservation right away."
- "Where would you like that shipped?"
- "It sounds like we've covered all your questions thoroughly, so let's discuss final terms."
- "If you don't have any more questions, let's talk about which model will be best for you."
- "I think you can see clearly now that the benefit outweighs the risk."
- "It sounds like you agree on the value of this product. I'm sure you'll agree how much greater the value is than the cost."
- "If I've answered all your questions, let's move on to see how we can make you the proud owner."

- "I can see that you now appreciate the value here. The next step is to discuss the terms."
- "We've agreed on the benefit and the value. Now let's agree on the final terms."
- "Do you have any more questions before we sign the contract?"

Closing the Deal: Asking for "Yes"

Sales-Success Mindsets

- An effective technique is to close with a simple yes/no question that is phrased to encourage a positive response, a "Yes" to accepting the deal, signing the contract, and moving ahead.
- Any time you ask for a "Yes," the answer might be "Yes." If you want to hear a "Yes," be bold about asking questions.
- Even if that question doesn't close the deal, the more yes's you get along the way, the more you will be leading to a positive response.
- Often, closing lines are suggested after responding to specific objections.
- You may hear a few no's before you hear "Yes." You also may hear a few yes's. Encourage them to build a positive mood.

Phrases

- "Would you like to start enjoying the benefits today?"
- "Are you ready to get started?"
- "Shall I draw up a contract?"
- "Great! Do we have a deal?"
- "I'm glad you're so excited about it! I think this will be a great fit for you! Should I draw up a contract?"
- "Do you think that this product or service will be beneficial to you and/or your clients?"
- "In order to accomplish the goals you've outlined, we would need an investment of $ _____. Are you ready to fill out the paperwork?"
- "Would you like to go ahead with this today?"

Closing the Deal: The A or B Close

Sales-Success Mindsets

■ Sometimes, offering a choice helps to initiate the close.

■ The A or B close presents a different choice from yes or no. It presents two options that are both yes.

■ A or B could represent a delivery date, a color, one line of products or another—anything that presents the final question as a choice.

■ A and B closings are an easy way to ask for the close.

■ These closings will sound obvious and pushy if repeated several times, even if you're changing the A and B.

■ The A or B close might include other options, too, but a decision is usually easier when choosing between two.

■ Instead of asking for a yes or no, you're asking, "Which one?"

Phrases

■ "Which color do you prefer? Okay, should I go ahead and order that for you in red?"

■ "Would you like to have this delivered to your home or your office?"

■ "What would be the most convenient delivery day for you, Friday or Saturday?"

■ "Would you prefer to finance through your bank or look at our financing options?"

■ "Yes, I can see why you like this view/this color/this model. What about this other one? No, I can see that the first one is really the one you want, isn't it? Shall we go ahead and order that for you?"

- "We have both the newer models available. Which would you prefer?"

- "The two models you were looking at are both available. Which one would you like?"

- "I can see why it's hard to make a decision with so many choices. Which would be your top two? What's most important to you? Of those two, which most meets your needs? Why? Great! Would you like me to go ahead and order that one for you?"

- "I have A available now, but I can order B and have it to you within a week. Which would you prefer?"

- "Will you be paying with by cash, check, or credit card?"

- "Should we order the deluxe package for you or the regular?"

- "Would you like to start with a box or a case?"

Closing the Deal: Touching Sense and Emotion

Sales-Success Mindsets

■ Most sales are made based on emotion.

■ Use every sense you can in the close: Let your prospects hear, see, and touch—encourage them to talk about what they like about it and how it will create positive feelings or outcomes for them, their families, or their businesses.

■ Help people to visualize positive outcomes.

■ Use words such as *imagine, feel,* and *visualize.*

■ If you're selling a product, always let people sample, if you can.

■ Touch is a sensational way to drive home the feel of having, using, or enjoying your product.

■ If you've passed around a sample of your product earlier in the presentation, let your prospects feel it again at the close.

■ If you're a storyteller, use your skills to sell the story of your prospects happily using or enjoying the benefits of your product or service.

■ People are emotional about losing an opportunity. The high-pressure buy-now-or-you-lose-the-deal close is transparent and will turn many prospects off. But if there's any truth in the fact that the deal will not be there or the price will go up or that model might change to something less appealing, let your prospects know.

■ Certain issues are highly emotional. If your sale affects security, education, or wellness, people will be highly

➡

invested in hearing what you have to say, but you may have to use emotional language to remind them of the importance of it or the impact on their families.

- If you can relate what you're selling directly to something close to home and heart, then you'll have a greater impact.

- Listening helps you to know what's most important to the prospect.

- If you're selling financial services and you know that your client has a child and is particularly interested in his or her education, don't just show how much can be saved or earned. Show how the extra money can be spent on that child's education. Use the child's name. Use as many specifics as you can. You're painting a picture of how that profit will help the prospect to achieve the goals and desires closest to his or her heart.

Phrases

- "Can you see where this would save you money/thrill your family/help your staff/inspire your creativity/bring you peace of mind? Are you ready to start saving money/thrilling your family/helping your staff/being inspired/enjoying peace of mind?"

- "You can take your chances by not buying now, but the price will go up. I received a notice of price increases on June 1, so you do have a little time. But if you're thinking of buying, you'll save money by buying now."

- "You've already expressed that you like it and it's within your price range. The only question is when you want to start enjoying the benefits!"

- "I can see your face light up when you think about taking advantage of all the amenities. This really is the best resort/time-share opportunity/vacation spot/on-site solution/spa/retreat center you can choose—and you deserve the best, don't you?"

- "If this service could save you a few hours each week or help you to completely free up your weekends, what would you do with the time?"

- "How do you envision your retirement? Most people either cannot retire when they want to or don't have the extra money to do all they dreamed of doing and have to focus on being careful to keep expenses down to the basics. What do you dream of doing when you retire? Can you see how this investment could make that picture a reality?"

- "This is a decision an intelligent person makes who cares about his/her family. I can tell you're an intelligent person, and I can tell that you care about your family."

- "I know you're concerned about the future well-being of your family. This decision will represent that to them."

- "It's always natural to feel nervous before jumping into the pool, but you have nothing to worry about here."

- "I respect your hesitancy in committing. I would do the same. The regret you're worrying about now will be nothing compared with the regret you'll feel if you don't act today."

Follow Up to Close the Sale

Sales-Success Mindsets

■ You will likely leave with questions or requests to address after the meeting.

■ Jot down notes in the moment. It's easy to think that you'll remember later—and so easy to forget.

■ If you're having trouble finding the answer, be prompt anyway in letting your prospect know about the delay. People will appreciate a call to say that you don't have an answer yet, but not hearing anything from you when expected will create bad feelings and can easily lose a sale.

■ People want to know in the case of a large sale or an ongoing account.

■ Be available and responsive, and keep your word.

■ If you say that you'll do something, do it. If you cannot, acknowledge that you cannot, and apologize. You may think that it's a small detail, but you're building trust—and there are no details too small when you're letting someone know that you can be counted on to follow through.

■ Say how long you expect it will be before you can get back to the prospect with an answer. If it's taking longer, follow up when you've said that you would to say what the slowdown is about and what the new estimated time is that you will have the information.

■ When it comes to following up, remember the adage: "Treat others as you would want to be treated." Let common sense and common courtesy be your guide. Don't assume that customers are busy and don't notice that you're not getting back to them in time. You'd notice if you were the prospective client—and what would *you* think of the salesperson who didn't follow up when he or she promised to?

Phrases

- "I'm having trouble finding that answer but wanted to get back to you to let you know that I'm doing my best to track it down. I expect to know by the end of the week and will call you by then."

- "I'll get back to you as soon as I find out. Feel free to call me in the meantime if you have any other questions."

- "I'm sorry I wasn't able to send those additional promotional toys for your kids yet. We have more coming in later in the week, and I'll be sure to get them right over to you. You said that they'd like a red and a blue, right?"

- "I'm sorry I don't have those figures for you yet. I forwarded the request to my partner, who had some additional questions in order to give you the most accurate answer. Do you have a moment?"

- "Here is the information you requested. Do you have any other questions you'd like answered?"

- "I found out the rest of the information we needed. Can I come in sometime this week to discuss it with you?"

Feel-Good Closing Words

Sales-Success Mindsets

- Always make your customer feel like he or she has made a good decision.

- Welcome prospects to your company's family.

- Let them know that this is the start of a positive relationship.

- Make them feel like they've made an investment, not a purchase.

- Make them feel like family members, not customers.

- Stress that they'll experience the benefits over time.

- The close of the sale is the beginning of the relationship.

- Replace their fear with faith.

- Replace their doubt with trust.

- Make them feel safe, appreciated, and special.

Phrases

- "We welcome you to our family of satisfied customers."

- "You've made a wise decision."

- "You've just become the proud owner of one of the finest products out there."

- "Your decision reflects your belief in quality over just price."

- "Your decision shows that you're a discriminating consumer."

- "I knew when I first saw you that you were an intelligent consumer."

➡

- "You've impressed me with your understanding of the process. I think that you'll be very happy with your decision."
- "I consider you a friend, not just a customer."
- "Our commitment to you has just begun."
- "We look forward to a successful, satisfying, long-term relationship."
- "You walked in a customer, and now you're part of our extended family."
- "You'll experience benefits today that will continue for a long time."
- "The benefits will resonate for years to come."
- "You didn't make a purchase. You made an investment for life."
- "The returns on your investment will compound for years to come."
- "As with any good investment, your purchase will produce dividends for years to come."
- "We're ending the transaction and beginning a friendship."

The Absolute Wrong Fit

Sales-Success Mindsets

- The best sale never made can be your best advertisement.

- Be honest—*always*.

- If you lose the sale because of your honesty, you'll build a reputation for integrity that will gain more sales in the long run—and a more successful career than you could ever build without it.

- Learn when to let go. Not only will you waste your prospect's time or create a bad relationship if it truly is a bad fit, but you'll also waste your own time.

- Never make anyone feel as though time spent seems wasted to you. Treat even those people who are no longer viable prospects as you would a valued customer. Show appreciation for any time that was given to you.

- Leave cards behind, and ask whether the would-have-been prospect would consider mentioning you to others who might be in the market and, if appropriate, remembering you if he or she is ever in need of or interested in your product or service in the future.

- If this isn't an appropriate time but there might be one in the future, ask if you can reach out again in a few months. If people encourage you to call again, they'll remember and almost always appreciate that you call back when they asked you to. Even though you're selling, they usually appreciate that you remember them.

- If you put in hours pursuing someone who's not a good prospect for what you have to offer, the time you waste is not only your prospect's—but your own as well.

Phrases

- "I can see that this isn't the best fit for you right now. Thank you for taking the time to meet with me and explore these options."

- "I understand where you're coming from. I don't want to try to sell you something that you don't need or that won't make you happy in the long run. Thank you for your time."

- "I understand your position. Thanks for meeting with me. Do you know anyone else who might be interested?"

- "Thank you for your time. Would you mind passing along my card/giving me a few names I could contact/making an e-mail introduction or two?"

- "I'm glad we had the opportunity to meet. Best of luck to you!"

- "May I leave you with a few cards in case it's of interest in the future or you know anyone now who might benefit from this service/product?"

- "I realize that this isn't the right time for you to consider this. Is it okay if I call you in a few months?"

- "I'm sorry we won't be working together, but it was a pleasure meeting you!"

- "Well, at least we've made a friend!"

- "If there's ever anything I can do for you in the future, please don't hesitate to call."

- "Can I leave a few cards on the counter in case any of your customers could use my services?"

- "Mind if I stop back again to say hello in a few months? Maybe you'll be interested. If not, I can at least have a chance to see what's new in your store."

- "Thanks again for speaking with me. Do you mind if I keep you on my e-mail list in case you might be interested in the future?"

- "I'll leave you with my card just in case. I appreciate your time. Thanks again."

Chapter 10

Follow-Up and Beyond

"The sale begins when the customer says *yes.*"
—Harvey MacKay

Following up is an important part of the process. You've made the sale. Now follow up to find out that products and/or services were delivered/installed/executed to the client's satisfaction. Show that you care and that the customer's satisfaction is as important to you as you said it would be when you were making the sale. Don't let, "I care," "I'll be with you every step of the way," or "Don't worry, you can count on me" sound like they were only empty promises in the end or, worse yet, lies you tell to make a sale. Beyond ensuring that the process went smoothly and that the customer is happy, maintaining the relationship is part of laying the groundwork for an ongoing relationship and future sales. Now, when you call, you're not another salesperson, but a trusted provider. When you follow up, you'll not only be continuing a positive interaction with your customers, but you'll also have an opportunity to ask for testimonials and referrals.

Follow Up after the Sale

Sales-Success Mindsets

■ Once you're following up, you're in the customer-care mode, making sure that your clients are happy and keeping doors open for additional sales.

■ Following up should be soon after, but create a schedule for periodically checking in. Eventually, it will be time for an upgrade or a change, or you might just catch someone at a moment when he or she will say, "What perfect timing! I could use . . ."

■ Create a process for sending periodic product/service updates and advice through newsletters (online/hardcopy), postcards, or e-mail.

■ Send out updates, keeping clients apprised of company news and special offers.

■ Ask for feedback. Encourage not only positive feedback but also any thoughts or concerns that would lead you to refine the service or make any corrections or changes along the way.

■ You also would rather have a chance to offer a change or something to make up for a difficulty than not know that the client is unhappy. (If you don't ask, the client may talk to others or even return/cancel your product/service without your ever having a chance to rectify the problem!)

■ Keep a calendar of special events such as birthdays. Birthday cards are a friendly way to keep in touch.

■ It's all about relationships!

- Following up is a great opportunity to collect feedback, testimonials, and referrals—and even to plant the seeds for future sales.

Phrases

- "Was everything delivered on time/installed to your satisfaction/as you expected it would be?"

- "How is the product/service/solution working out for you?"

- "Are you satisfied?"

- "What works well?"

- "What challenges have surfaced?"

- "Would you be interested in filling out a feedback profile so that we can continue to provide the best possible service?"

- "Hi. Just wanted to follow up to see how things are going."

- "What new solutions can we provide?"

- "I'm glad things are going so well! We have some new offerings, and I'd love to get together to show you what's new! Can I take you to lunch sometime next week?"

- "Now that you're experiencing the benefits already, would you like to schedule ahead for the future? We're already booking up, and I'd always prefer to give existing clients priority scheduling."

- "Thank you for continuing to grow with us!"

Ask for Feedback

Sales-Success Mindsets

- Don't let too much time pass. Excitement may wane, and people get busy.
- Encourage honest feedback.
- If you have your own feedback form, always leave a space for general comments.
- On the form itself, ask whether comments may be used for promotional purposes, and provide space for a signature if the answer is yes.
- Consider reaching out through a third-party service for feedback. People will be more likely to give answers that are candid and completely honest.
- Embrace negative feedback. It can help you to redirect your approach and make changes that ultimately will increase your sales.

Phrases

- "You'll be receiving a feedback form. I hope you'll take a few moments to fill it out. I would appreciate any feedback from you about your experience working with us."
- "Thank you for the positive feedback! Would you mind writing a few words of endorsement?"
- "Please be honest in your feedback evaluation, and don't worry about my feelings. Any feedback you give will help me and my colleagues to provide you with better service."

- "I'm sorry that you didn't have the best experience. What can I do to make things right?"

- "It's a very good product, and I'd appreciate the opportunity to work with you if you decide it's right for you."

- "I'm sorry to hear about your experience with our service department. That never should have happened. I'm going to follow up with them and see what they can do for you to make up for that inconvenience."

- "Thank you! I'm so pleased that you're happy."

- "Thank you for your thoughtful response to our survey. I found it extremely helpful. It's such a pleasure to be working with you!"

Ask for Referrals and Testimonials

Sales-Success Mindsets

- When results are strong, don't delay. Ask for referrals and/or a testimonial.

- Happy customers will be glad to help you.

- When you help others, they generally feel good about helping you in return.

- If you've shown that you're trustworthy and you've delivered what the customer wants, that customer will want those he or she works with and/or cares about to have the same good service, positive benefits, and personal care that you've shown that you provide.

- No one wants to recommend someone who might not do the right thing for those to whom they'd make a recommendation.

Phrases

- "I'm so excited by the positive results you've had! Would you mind offering a testimonial?" (Immediately give the format you require with a reasonable deadline. People have the best intentions, but a testimonial easily can be back-burnered and ultimately forgotten.)

- "If you believe that my product/service/solution would benefit any of your colleagues, would you mind sending out an e-mail introduction linking to me?"

- "Do you know of any other people I might be able to work with? Do you mind if I jot down their names and contact information?"

- "Thank you for the referrals! I'll let you know what happens."

- "You mentioned someone else who might be interested. Would you consider making a phone introduction?"

- "Thank you for the referrals! I appreciate the trust you showed in passing along my name. I'll keep you in the loop and let you know what happens."

- "Thank you so much for your kind words. I love what I do and how I can have the opportunity to help others, and I'm glad to know that it shows."

Part Three

Ongoing Development

Chapter 11

Eleven Final Thoughts on Learning

"You can't cross the sea merely by standing and staring at the water."

—Rabindranath Tangore

Great salespeople are always learning and honing their skills as they continue to forge and nurture great client relationships. Salespeople are multitalented multitaskers and never have a shortage of new and exciting things to learn or skills to practice. Salespeople are public speakers, professional listeners, and negotiators, and they are savvy about service and psychology. Industries, markets, companies, technologies, demographics, and even the way we do business change all the time. The tried-and-true essentials of communication are fundamental growth tools that we develop continually throughout our lives and careers. Salespeople who are always learning are always in demand.

1. Practice Active Learning

With any self-improvement and professional development program, practice is the key. The more you actively participate in any program, the more you'll learn. If there's a workbook, an exercise, or any suggestions along the way for journaling, surveying, or trying out any new skill, don't delay. Learning programs will have more of an impact if you're an active learner. The impact is far greater if you participate as you listen, watch, or read. To really make new ideas a part of your consciousness and integrate them into your life, you have to think about them and put them into practice in a conscious, intentional way. No one's approach will be exactly right for you, but recognize your successes and modify as you see fit.

2. Study, Learn, and Practice Public Speaking

Continue to hone your speaking skills. If you have stress or fear associated with getting up in front of a room, remember that you might be standing up there alone, but you're not at all alone in feeling that way. Survey after survey shows public speaking as the number one fear, even above death. Some sum it up and point out just how extreme the fear is by saying that people at a funeral would rather be in the casket than giving the eulogy! If you have these fears, you may alleviate them partially or altogether, permanently or not—even some of the most talented speakers and actors still suffer panic attacks or have to actively tame the fear before public appearances. So, will the fear ever go away? There's no telling. But we do know that we can tame fears and put them in their proper perspective.

Self-help books and programs are wonderful, and so is one-to-one coaching or working the issue through with any professional who deals with fears. The important thing is to know that it's not something you have to fix before you can be successful. You're not broken; you just suffer from a common fear—one that most often is tamed by repeated positive experiences. Listen to great speakers and inspirational talks. Read about public speaking, and implement each new idea you hear. And practice, practice, practice! Increase your comfort with speaking by pursuing a few speaking engagements, joining Toastmasters International, and even trying out your presentation on a few trusted colleagues. Public speaking is the greatest fear for many. Whether you need to increase your comfort level or hone your skills or both, take every opportunity to practice.

Following are some helpful speaking resources:

- Toastmasters International (http://toastmasters.org).
- Miller, Anne, *Metaphorically Selling*, (Chiron Associates, 2004).
- Reynolds, Garr, *Presentation Zen: Simple Ideas on Presentation Design and Delivery (Voices That Matter)*, (New Riders, 2007).
- Sjodin, Terri L., *New Sales Speak: The 9 Biggest Sales Presentation Mistakes and How to Avoid Them*, (John Wiley & Sons, Inc., 2006).
- Tracy, Brian, *Speak to Win: How to Present with Power in Any Situation*, (AMACOM, 2008).

3. Strengthen Your Writing Skills

Is your writing style clear and concise? Do you know how to avoid common grammar and spelling errors? What do your written words say about you? Your writing says volumes about your style, professionalism, and attention to detail. Much emphasis is placed on image in sales from materials to clothes and even to cars and, of course—since we are discussing phrases here—the spoken word. Although many people place more emphasis on the spoken word than the written word, the written (or typed) word is more permanent and may be passed along to others.

Beyond image, good writing is more effective. You might think writing is not that important to your clients, letters, e-mails, and proposals that are well written are more reader-friendly and easier to review and comprehend. When working to improve your writing, you can easily find some good tips for persuasive writing. Even if your written contact with prospects and clients is minimal, make it the best you can.

If you don't want to hone your writing skills, hire someone to write for you. Either way, remember that your written image is important and that careful writing shows the kind of attention to detail that you want your prospects and clients to see.

Following are some helpful writing resources:

- Debelak, Don, *Perfect Phrases for Business Proposals and Business Plans*, (New York: McGraw-Hill, 2005).
- Diamond, Harriet, Diamond, Linda Eve, and Fahey, Marsha, *Executive Writing: American Style,* (Berkeley: Apocryphile Press, 2007).
- Diamond, Harriet, and Dutwin, Phyllis, *Writing the Easy Way*, (New York: Barron's Educational Series, 2000).
- O'Quinn, Ken, *Perfect Phrases for Business Letters,* (New York: McGraw-Hill, 2005).

4. Always Be Learning to Listen

Much like selling, listening is both a skill and an art, and it is also the foundation of all interactions—both business and personal. In sales, listening is the most essential skill you can develop. You can hone your tactics and your phrases, perfect the nuts and bolts of perfect closings—but if you're not listening, you're far less likely to be successful in sales. What do your prospects want? How can you sell them anything if you don't know? And why would they buy anything from someone who isn't listening and showing an interest in offering the best product or service for their needs? How can you better comprehend prospects' needs so that you can solve problems and find solutions for more sales and happy customers? *Listen*!

Following are some helpful listening resources:

- Diamond, Linda Eve, *Rule #1: Stop Talking! A Guide to Listening*, (Silicon Valley: Listeners Press, 2007); also available as an e-book at http://LindaEveDiamond.com.
- Listeners Unite! (http://ListenersUnite.com)
- The International Listening Association (ILA) (http://Listen.org)

5. Listen, Watch, and Read the Work of Great Motivators

Why are motivational seminars so popular among salespeople? Salespeople can't survive without them. Rejection is especially difficult for most people. For salespeople, it's just part of the day, but still we're only human. Sometimes we need to be reminded of how to have the superhuman strength to keep going in the face of rejection and to remember that it's all a numbers game. Read motivational books, listen in your car, and catch a seminar when you can. If you're looking for a *perfect phrase* to keep you going, there's no shortage of motivational messages.

Following are some helpful motivational resources:

- Covey, Stephen, *The 7 Habits of Highly Effective People,* (Simon & Schuster Adult, 2004).
- Johnson, Jim, *The Sixty-Second Motivator,* (Dog Ear Publishing, 2006).
- Reeve, Johnmarshall, *Understanding Motivation and Emotion,* (John Wiley & Sons, Inc., 2008).
- Robbins, Anthony, *Awaken the Giant Within: How to Take Immediate Control of Your Mental, Emotional, Physical and Financial Destiny!,* (Simon & Schuster Adult, 1991).

6. Keep Up to Speed with Your Professional Development

Keep up with your industry and the industries with which you deal on a regular basis. Keep up with journals, professional associations, current events, and economic forecasts. Beyond keeping up with and honing your sales skills, you need to be informed about news and events within and related to your industry. Whatever you're selling, at the heart of every sale you are educating and advising. You may change industries from time to time, but wherever you are at any given time, immerse yourself. Know your field, and you'll increase your value and have an endless supply to draw on of *perfect phrases* for any sales situation within your given industry. Only you know the best Web sites, journals, trade magazines, and other resources for keeping informed about your industry.

7. Study, Watch, Learn, and Practice Sales Skills

All the resources in this section are helpful for sales. Then, of course, so are specific resources for learning, honing, and developing the art of selling. Resources abound. Some names are famous in sales, and they're famous for a reason. Immerse yourself in books, CDs, and DVDs by Zig Ziglar, Brian Tracy, and Anthony Robbins, and you'll notice yourself making at least subtle improvements and refinements. You can easily find countless articles online about sales from top salespeople and magazines and even some blogs that you might only discover by searching for answers or ideas about a specific sales topic. You also can find sales associations and online communities, forums, discussions, and groups.

Here are just a few sales resources:

- Brooks, William T., *Perfect Phrases for the Sales Call,* (McGraw-Hill, 2005).
- Futrell, Charles M., *Fundamentals of Selling*, (McGraw-Hill, 2004).
- Hopkins, Tom, Waitley, Denis, Widener, Chris, and Ziglar, Zig, *Sales Success: Motivation from Today's Top Sales Coaches*, (Audio CD, Audio Success Series), (XX: Topics Entertainment, 2004).
- Ziglar, Zig, *Secrets of Closing the Sale*, (Penguin Group, 1985).

Sales is a fascinating career in that it incorporates many aspects of performance creativity and human nature. If you have any interest in psychology, problem solving, and creative thinking, any resources in those areas are also extremely helpful in sales. The sale itself also has a number of different aspects. For instance, volumes have been written on closings alone.

8. Keep Up with Technology

Keep up with technology, but don't let it overtake your presentation. Create an attractive presentation that shows that you're up to speed with the times; use technology as a tool to best convey your message, but don't let technology overwhelm your message or have all your resources locked up in a presentation in a way that a technical glitch can hopelessly separate you from your information. Have your most important points with you as notes, not just on your computer. Always be prepared for technical failures and have backups and even backups for your backups. Of course, if all else fails, the most powerful backup is a strong knowledge base about your industry, your product or service, and your prospect.

9. Keep Up a Strong Knowledge Base

Even if everything goes wrong—the equipment's not working, the samples are in your lost luggage, you spot your competition's promotional material and think it puts yours to shame—you still have the basics: You know your product, you know your prospect, and you genuinely care to create a good fit and a happy customer. Remember that backup material is important and should strongly represent you, but how you carry yourself when things go wrong and how comfortable you can make your prospect are the most important elements of your presentation. Backup enhances—use it and use it well. However, if you're well prepared, you'll be fine with or without it.

10. Use the Buddy System

Another way to enhance your learning is to share these ideas with others. Learn together, and learn from each other. Discussing what you hear and even explaining concepts to one another will help to deepen your understanding and awareness immeasurably. Find a "success buddy"—someone who's also interested in improving and succeeding in the same ways—and help each other grow. Beyond the added benefits to learning, it will make the process more fun and enhance a friendship, partnership, or relationship as you continue to inspire each other.

Remember, it's the "buddy system" and not the "competitive-edge club." Efforts to outdo each other and show each other up are counterproductive. Some people like this kind of competitive game, but in the end, isn't it more demotivating than motivating? You're focusing on achieving success and learning the importance of positive language and thinking—so don't infuse the process with negative overtones. No one is positively inspired by feeling demoralized. Don't be afraid to be positive, inspiring, and supportive—and to accept the same in return. If this makes you uncomfortable, you may consider that whatever it is that makes that uncomfortable for you—a comfort level with negative language, a self-limiting belief system, a self-worth issue—these very things can hold you back in the areas in which you're trying to grow. If giving and sharing positive reinforcement are not the most natural state for you, the buddy system itself might be an important part of your learning process.

11. Be a Student of Life, School, and Beyond

Beyond continuing to learn in any or all of the 10 ways listed above, we're always learning about ourselves and the people around us. We can choose to let things go by without taking them in, but the more we watch and care to learn, the more we learn. Most great salespeople have a good sense of people and are interested in learning about themselves, the world around them, and human nature. A salesperson can be great without any formal education just by being a student of human nature out in the world. Depending on what you sell, where you sell, what certificates or degrees might be required in your industry, or what your prospects value or expect, your education may or may not be important. Even if you have advanced degrees and extensive certifications, your degree of knowledge about life and your understanding of people are what will connect you to others and create strong, profitable business relationships with clients and potential clients.

Formal degrees and certifications will gain you a level of respect and will be required to different degrees and may elevate your status and open more doors. You should, of course, have the minimum required or expected in terms of degrees or certifications for your field, industry, and circle of prospects.

Ongoing Development

If you go beyond and have additional degrees or certifications, you can only help your status and strengthen your professional bio. Education strengthens you in every area of your life, sparks your brain, charges up your interest, raises new questions, and broadens and deepens you as a person. Ongoing formal learning may not be required, but if it will improve your standing and you can make it work, don't hesitate. Even if a specific course doesn't lead to a certification or degree, it will add to the richness of your knowledge base. The return on your investment in an individual course may come in a particular sales situation, or it may come in affecting your underlying beliefs or understanding in an area that will affect who and where you are in your life as well as in your career.

Any seminars or courses, especially in any aspect of the selling mindset or process or in any of the areas that are foundational for a strong sales career, such as speaking, writing, listening, psychology, or motivation, will have an impact on your bottom line. Beyond that, learn everything you can that strengthens your knowledge base within your industry and particularly about your product or service. If selling is a transfer of enthusiasm, the enthusiasm begins with you. If you can be enthusiastic about your product or service, your industry, your growth, your life—your clients will feel that enthusiasm, too. They will enjoy your presence, your knowledge, your input, and your relationship with them. Learn what you can about being a great salesperson, but also learn anything you can that will make you more knowledgeable, personable, empathetic, and friendly, and you'll become a greater salesperson along the way.

Chapter 12

Your *Perfect Phrases*

"The *perfect phrase* for your sales presentation!"
—You

Have You Made *Perfect* Notes?

Hopefully, you will continue to use the *perfect phrases* from this book that apply, modify others, and use these phrases as foundations for creating your own *perfect phrases*. As you read, you've probably already come up with a few of your own. To engrain them in your memory and have them handy as you create presentations or enter into networking and sales situations, you may have highlighted, tabbed, and jotted down phrases of particular interest to you.

What Makes a Phrase *Perfect*?

What makes a phrase *perfect*? What makes it meaningful or effective? There is no magic recipe for creating the *perfect phrase,* just a dose of introspection, a dash of understanding the other person, and a good helping of thoughts behind the words you sprinkle in to create the phrase.

A *Perfect* Brainstorm

Now let's take another step and brainstorm some new *perfect phrases.* You may do this over time, but in a notebook or document, brainstorm your own *perfect phrases* for each of the following, making each bullet the heading of a page and adding as many phrases as you can:

- Cold-call openings
- Opening lines at networking events
- The best first line for your presentation
- The best last line for your presentation
- The best answer to the most common objection you hear
- The best answers to other objections you might anticipate
- Great closings for your sales presentations (might include great quotes or relevant statistics)
- Great phrases for closing the sale
- Great metaphors relating to what you're selling
- Stories that provide good threads to be woven through interesting presentations

When you feel you've run out of phrases, push yourself to come up with three more. You may be surprised by the creativity that surfaces just when you think the well is dry. Once you've completed the exercise, more may come to you later in the day or over time, as you're driving, in the midst of a presentation, or while you're doing something completely different. Jot them down, and add them to your lists. Keep these lists alive and active, referring to and adding to this book and your lists over time. You'll find that your new phrases will become engrained, and your presentations will continually refine.

A *Perfect* Buddy

Do you know someone else who might have ideas to contribute? Take your brainstorming to a new level by going through the process with someone else in your field. Share your lists, and see how many more entries you can come up with together. Write them all down—even the silly ones. The more fun you have, the more great, usable ideas you'll generate by the end. Then you can practice them, share them with your phrase-generating buddy, and see what worked well and what you might refine. You don't have to make a job out of it or take it too seriously, but if you allow yourself to have a perfectly good time playing with phrases, you might just find an opener that opens more doors, a closing line that gets them nearly every time, or a great story that sparks your prospects' imaginations and entices them to invest in your product or service.

More *Perfect Phrase* Tips

Perfectly Positive

Most *perfect phrases* have a positive tone. As you develop and refine your phrases, use positive words and positive feelings. Go through your phrases, and flag negative words such as *not, aren't, can't,* and *won't*. Can you rephrase with a positive tone? For example, change "Our widgets aren't flimsy" to "Our widgets are strong" or "The strength and durability of our widgets are the backbone of our success." Instead of "It's not uncommon for our consulting clients to cut employee turnover by as much as 50 percent," say, "Our clients cut employee turnover by as much as 50 percent" or "Our clients retain as much as 50 percent more of their valued employees."

Think in positive words and positive terms. Is your success not uncommon or is it common? It may be the same thing, but cutting the negative words gives the phrase a more positive sound. Is your glass half empty or is it half full? Is the prospect half disinterested or half interested? Are your words not uninspiring or are they inspiring? Be *perfectly* positive for a positively *perfect* outcome.

Perfectly Clear

Language is the stuff of which your phrase is made—use it wisely. Language involves a number of choices. The language we choose for communication matters should be clear and concise. Problems arise when we use words unfamiliar to the listener, whether there is a language barrier or we are simply enjoying our new-word-a-day calendar at the expense of anyone who chose a Dilbert calendar instead. We also lose each other with technical jargon and Internet shorthand.

Cross-cultural communications also require that we be careful of using too many idioms. These expressions, unique to our own language and culture, make no sense in direct translation and can leave someone who is less familiar with our language in the dark. They won't know what you did last night if say you "went on a bender" and "tied one on." Many can be figured out by context and tone, but others can't, and if you string a bunch together, they surely will put you out on a limb.

Perfect Tone

If someone doesn't see your sarcasm, your phrase will be interpreted as the exact opposite of what you intended. If you love sarcasm, don't play it straight. Let people in on the joke with a smile! Again, even that can be misconstrued. Sarcasm on a sales call or during a sales presentation should be used with caution and obvious humor.

Perfect Body Language

The overall tone of your message is affected by nonverbal factors as well. Your body sometimes speaks for itself. Be careful not to defy your own careful phrasing with your body's language. You can say, "I know you need my attention right now; I'm listening," but if you're inviting questions and then flipping through your notes while being asked, you're not connecting with the prospects and showing that you're listening.

Perfect Phrases

You have, in this book, hundreds of *perfect phrases* and the means to keep *perfect phrasing* in mind as you continue to develop and refine your sales presentations. Remember that the most *perfect phrase* is always the one that shows that you're listening, that you care, and that you want the very best for your prospects, clients, and customers.

Conclusion

"If we did all the things we were capable of doing, we would literally astound ourselves."

—Thomas Edison

The world of sales is exciting and ever-changing, and your presentations will always continue to evolve. Finding *perfect phrases* for perfect sales presentations is an imperfect process—but that's part of the challenge, the process, and the fun. As you continue to refine your presentations, I hope that you will incorporate and modify these *perfect phrases* and continue to create your own *perfect phrases* based on your product and prospect and the changing times.

I suggest keeping, along with this book and among your other personal development and sales tools, a *perfect phrase* journal that includes the phrases you developed in going through Chapter 12. You also may have highlighted phrases and tabbed some of the pages of *Perfect Phrase for Sales Presentations* on which you found the most useful phrases for you (whether in their original forms or with modifications). You might want to copy some of those into your *perfect phrase* journal to have the most useful ones all in the same place. The book will, I hope, remain on your shelf for reference in future situations. But the phrases that are needed most are the ones you'd want to focus on first and incorporate into your calls and presentations. The more you focus on the preciseness and power of your words, the more your off-the-cuff phrases will become targeted, meaningful, and *perfect* for the situation.

Also, as you deepen your listening awareness and notice how listening affects your business relationships and your sales, you'll learn the value of simply listening. Of equal importance to the *perfect phrase* is being a *perfect listener*. Are we really perfect at either one? Maybe some days, but no one is perfect all the time at either speaking or listening. Speaking—developing the *perfect phrase* and the *perfect presentation*—and listening—to discover the client's needs, concerns, objections, fears, and values—are both practices that we can improve over time, and we do improve overall with noticeable results. I hope that you are *perfectly* happy with the results you achieve as you put into practice your *perfect phrases* and that you will give the process your time and attention. You may think that you don't have time to focus on your phrases once you put this book down, but time is a small investment for any new practice that might benefit your bottom line. And wouldn't that, in the end, buy you more time?

I think that any book or concept applied actively produces more change and results than one that is read or referenced, although we always walk away from any helpful book with something new that becomes a part of our thinking. However, of course, the book also works well, as all *perfect phrase* books do, as something helpful to skim and a handy reference to carry or keep on your shelf. As always, *perfect phrase* books are jumping off points, reminders, touchstones, and idea generators, especially if you take advantage of the guidelines for developing your own. Remember also that beyond the phrases you find or develop, if you have knowledge and a genuine interest in your prospect or client, you'll always have the *perfect phrase*.

About the Author

inda Eve Diamond is the author of several books in the areas of education, self-help, motivation, team building, business writing, and poetry. Listening as a critical, learnable skill is a central theme throughout her diverse work. After writing and teaching communication skills in a corporate training setting for nearly 15 years, she decided to fine-tune her focus on communication by exploring the importance of listening—from the inner to the interpersonal—as essential for personal fulfillment and business success. She is the recipient of two 2008 International Listening Association Awards: "The President's Award" and the award for "Listening in the Business Sector." Also an award-winning poet, Linda shares her perspective on the art of listening through her creative works as well. She is available for speaking engagement and listening skills training that focuses on the power of listening in all contexts, including how to use listening to boost sales. Listening skills training can be customized to any organization or group.

Visit Linda Eve Diamond's regularly updated Web sites at http://LindaEveDiamond.com and http://ListenersUnite.com. Books by Linda Eve Diamond:

- *Rule #1: Stop Talking! A Guide to Listening* (Silicon Valley, CA: Listeners Press, 2007).

- *Executive Writing: American Style* (Berkeley, CA: Apocryphile Press, 2007).
- *TABE (Tests of Adult Basic Education) Level: A Verbal Workbook* (New York: McGraw-Hill, 2007).
- *Perfect Phrases for Building Strong Teams* (New York: McGraw-Hill, 2007).
- *Perfect Phrases for Motivating and Rewarding Employees* (New York: McGraw-Hill, 2006).
- *Teambuilding That Gets Results* (Naperville, IL: Sourcebooks, 2007).
- *The Human Experience* (New York: ASJA Press, 2007).